Developing
Family Business
Policies:
Your Guide to the Future

Craig E. Aronoff, Ph.D. ,
Joseph H. Astrachan, Ph.D. and
John L. Ward, Ph.D.

D1113063

Family Business Leadership Series, No. 11

Family Enterprise Publishers
P.O. Box 4356
Marietta, GA 30061-4356

ISSN: 1071-5010
ISBN: 1-891652-01-X

© 1998
Second Printing

Family Business Leadership Series

We believe that family businesses are special, not only to the families that own and manage them but to our society and to the private enterprise system. Having worked and interacted with hundreds of family enterprises in the past twenty years, we offer the insights of that experience and the collected wisdom of the world's best and most successful family firms.

This volume is a part of a series offering practical guidance for family businesses seeking to manage the special challenges and opportunities confronting them.

To order additional copies, contact:
Family Enterprise Publishers
1220-B Kennestone Circle
Marietta, Georgia 30066
Tel: 1-800-551-0633
Web Site: www.efamilybusiness.com

Quantity discounts are available.

Other volumes in the series include:

Family Business Succession: The Final Test of Greatness

Family Meetings: How to Build a Stronger Family and a Stronger Business

Another Kind of Hero: Preparing Successors For Leadership

How Families Work Together

Family Business Compensation

How to Choose & Use Advisors: Getting the Best Professional Family Business Advice

Financing Transitions: Managing Capital and Liquidity in the Family Business

Family Business Governance: Maximizing Family and Business Potential

Preparing Your Family Business For Strategic Change

Making Sibling Teams Work: The Next Generation

Developing Family Business Policies: Your Guide to the Future

Family Business Values: How to Assure a Legacy of Continuity and Success

More Than Family: Non-Family Executives in the Family Business

CONTENTS

EXHIBITS

I. Introduction:
A Wonderful Gift

Consider the Lawrence family, owners of a string of hardware stores in the Midwest. The members of the second generation and leaders of the business — two brothers and a sister and their spouses — invite all the family members to a big weekend retreat, and during the retreat, for the first time, the members of the third generation, ages 15 to 24, meet together.

Adrian Lawrence, CEO, explained to the family that businesses create policies to assure consistency, fairness and efficiency in decision making. "Rather than making lots of ad hoc decisions, they create policies to guide actions related to matters ranging from compensation to extending credit to customers," he said. Most businesses develop loose-leaf policy manuals to give managers a ready-reference aid to decision making. Adrian then passed around copies of the policy manual used in the family's business.

Adrian's sister-in-law, Jean Lawrence, Vice President, then picked up the discussion. "As we thought about the future of our family's business," she explained, "**we realized that we needed policies not just to guide decisions inside the business, but we needed policies to guide decisions about the relationship between the family and the business.** We were facing some very tough questions about pay, about how our children would enter and advance in the business, about how our board of directors would operate . . . and many more. If those decisions, which would be required many times in the future, were not seen as consistent and fair, the potential for disastrous family conflict was very evident."

"That's why we put together our family business policy guide," added Alex MacMillan, a brother-in-law who practiced dentistry, as individual copies of another bulky notebook were passed out to each family member. **"We believe that this book of policies to guide our family's decisions and actions in relation to the business and to each other contains the most important policies of all."**

Inside the three-ring binder, the young people found, in written form, all of the policies that the Lawrence family had created to guide and govern the family business — a family mission statement, a policy spelling out the rules for joining the family business, a shareholder agreement, a statement setting forth the family's beliefs about philanthropy, a code of conduct, and much more. It also included background on the discussion that went into each document so that

1

the third generation could see their parents' (and, in some cases, grand-parents') thought processes. It even included dissenting opinions.

The parents encouraged their children to read the manual carefully and discuss it among themselves, and to ask the parents any questions they might have. As one parent put it, "These are the rules of the game — our constitution, so to speak — with background information to help you understand why we came up with the rules we did. It will be up to you to review what we have done and, when the time comes, to revise the rules to fit the needs of the family and the business in your generation." That book was one of the best gifts that they could ever have given their children.

Most family businesses haven't worked as hard as the Lawrence clan to develop family business policies. (Like other families discussed in this booklet, the Lawrence family is fictitious, but based on real cases.) If you are like most family business owners, you probably have a basic will in place and, hopefully, a shareholder agreement. Perhaps you've thought it would be a good idea to put together some other documents and policies to guide the direction and management of your business, but you just haven't known how to go about doing it. Or it just seems too difficult to do, given how hard it is to get members of your family to agree on anything.

Policies do not just guide decisions inside the business, but guide decisions about the relationship between the family and the business.

But policy development cannot be put off forever. Sooner or later, every business family needs to formalize and set down on paper the structure and guidelines under which the family will own and operate their business. Why? We will explore the answers to that question in great detail in Chapter 2. But the simplest, quickest answer is that having agreed-upon policies in place and abiding by them reduce the chances that family conflicts will destroy your family business.

As advisors to the family business, our work is most beneficial when we are able to work with family businesses not facing immediate crises. The best family businesses recognize that they will eventually encounter stress and strain in family and business — so they prepare for it long before crisis hits. How does a family business best avoid problems? There are two possible answers:

1. By having extremely good luck.

2. By solving problems before they occur in an atmosphere free of major conflict. In other words, creating family business policies.

In this volume, we lay out what many successful family businesses do to help insure prosperity. They develop policies through a process that builds unity of vision, commitment, and good feelings about one another and about the business. These policies deal with a host of issues that family businesses typically face, provide solutions that all have agreed to before family conflict made agreement impossible. Successful business-owning families rarely wait until battle lines are drawn to resolve real and immediate problems. They understand that when family members are fighting, it is nearly impossible to set aside personal agendas or to overcome excessive emotionality.

In our view, **a family should solve problems before they happen**. Problems and conflicts are a natural, normal, predictable product of the evolution of a family business. We encourage family members to get together, talk things out and engage in planning as a means of anticipating and dealing with the problems that will inevitably occur. In many cases, the outcome of such planning is a decision that says, "When something like this happens, we will handle it this way." And that's called a policy.

Often, families create policies without realizing it or being thoughtful about it. **These policies aren't written, but take the form of powerful statements like: "That's the way Dad [or Mom] wanted it." "That's the way it has always been done around here." "That's how our family does it."** Particularly in the first generation, entrepreneurs may make decisions that they don't think of as policies — they're just seen as decisions. Such decisions can set precedents that become policies. In a sense, the founder embodies the policies. We encourage founders to recognize that their decisions can become precedents for generations to come.

The family that wants to extend its business to the next generation and generations beyond ultimately will find it necessary and useful to move beyond such casual, implicit setting of policy and to deliberately and explicitly create guidelines that will chart a successful course for the family and the business. This booklet will help you and your family do that — whether you are a founder and spouse thinking about issues related to the continuity of your business and family; a group of siblings and spouses considering how you will make decisions together about the future of your business and your family; or a member of a third- or fourth-generation business that

3

may need to expand, clarify or update family business policies.

Although we offer some samples of useful policies, **it is not our intent to have your family adopt any specific policy as it appears here or to hand you a set of policies and say, "use these." That would, as you will see in Chapter 2, deprive you and your family of the most important benefit of developing policies: going through the process of doing so.**

We are firm believers that, when it comes to creating and adopting a policy, no one size fits all. In other words, a policy that suits one family may not be right for another. The policies you need and their ultimate content depend on many factors, including the stage of your business, its corporate culture, the values and background of your family, and whether you are a family who puts family first or a family who puts business first.

It *is* our intent to guide you through a process that will enable your family (1) to determine what policies it needs at its present stage, and (2) to create those policies. We will do this by helping you to understand the rationales for certain policies and to look at the issues that different policies raise. We also offer thoughts about the implementation of policies, as well as guidelines for how often policies need to be re-visited and revised.

The policies you need and their ultimate content depend on many factors, including the stage of your business, its corporate culture, the values and background of your family, and whether you are a family who puts family first or a family who puts business first.

As you create and adopt the policies that are right for your family, you are, in essence, creating the "laws" that govern your family business. Once you begin formulating your policies, you can gather them together into a single manual, which everyone has access to and can refer to as needed. This will be your policy guide.

We urge you not to let policies develop haphazardly or without real consideration. Instead, we invite you to be thoughtful about their creation and to put in the effort that's required to take control of the process. It won't be easy work, but it will be some of the most rewarding work you have ever done. Your family and your business will be better for it, and you will be giving your children an incomparable gift.

II. *What Policy Making Can Do For Your Family and Your Business*

Policies governing the relationship between the family and the business are important to any family business. What is more important, however, is the *process* family members engage in when they create policies. We cannot emphasize that enough.

Developing policies requires that family members communicate with one another about difficult issues. It means letting go of past conflicts and hearing each other out respectfully in the here and now, as well as exhibiting a willingness to search for creative solutions and compromises. The process is laid out in more detail in Chapter 3.

Needless to say, many families know the process is complex and demanding, and that's why they put off developing the policies they need. But the families that plunge ahead reap the rewards and benefits provided by having policies in place and going through the process of creating them. Here are some of those benefits:

☛ **The policies themselves help families solve current and future problems.** As one family-business owner once told us, "I've learned that successful family businesses do a good job of anticipating future issues and talking about how to deal with them as a family *before* they become issues."

Consider these questions:

- "What happens if my brother thinks my nephew should be promoted, but I disagree?"

- "What happens if my cousin gives his wife company stock and then they get divorced?"

- "What happens if we have to fire a family member?"

- "With eleven family members on the board, shouldn't some be getting off?"

- "How can I tell my son that he needs to get more work experience before joining the family business?"

- "Even if I'm not in the business, I own shares. Why shouldn't I get the same financial information as family who *are* in the business?"

- "Why should your husband get paid more than mine?"

- "What do you mean, you took a $100,000 loan from the business?"

- "Why can't I be on the board?"

- "How can your son work in the family business and run another business at the same time?"
- "Shouldn't the business buy its group health policy from me? After all, I am family."

Such questions can be the stuff of family business nightmares. Agreeing on solutions to such problems in advance can depersonalize issues and insure greater objectivity.

☞ **Policies help avoid problems and conflicts before they happen. They eliminate or reduce future tension.** When families take the time to identify and discuss issues that might lead to future disagreement and tension, they are actually determining the most important areas in which policies might be needed.

Developing policies before they are needed creates an opportunity for families to address potentially sensitive issues before they become personalized — that is, before they actually apply to someone. In one business, for example, Justin was disturbed when his brother and father, without warning, demanded that he require his fiancee, Francine, to sign a prenuptial agreement. "She'll think that I'm planning for divorce or that, at the very least, I don't truly love her," he objected.

Justin's father and brother were both upset and could not convince him of the importance of a prenuptial agreement in protecting the business. He was finally persuaded, but only after much argument and coercion that still affect his relationships. And he was right about Francine. When he broached the subject with her, weeks of ill-feeling and argument followed. She finally signed because she loved Justin and wanted to please him, but to this day, she feels that Justin's father and brother do not like her.

Developing policies before they are needed creates an opportunity for families to address potentially sensitive issues before they become personalized — that is, before they actually apply to someone.

Contrast this to another case where a business owner was able to communicate effectively to Rose, his then 16-year-old daughter, that before she married, her husband-to-be would need to sign a prenuptial agreement. Rose had no vested interest and nothing to lose at that point, so she was able to hear what was being said about the value of such agreements and how they could protect the family and the business should an unwanted divorce ever occur. Rose is in her early 20s now and still single. But when she chooses to marry, Rose and her intended will know the rule and its purpose. They will also know that it long preceded their relationship, so neither will interpret the rule as a personal reflection on her choice of a mate.

Families who go through the policy-setting process actually affect expectations and therefore, we believe, moderate and possibly eliminate some of the prickly issues that typically arise in family businesses. Family members have already contemplated the issues, they know what the consequences will be, and they know what the family stance is on each. As a result of their deliberations and the fact that they have a good battery of policies in place before the need, sometimes the issues just don't even arise.

EXHIBIT 1: ██

Reasons to Develop a Policy Guide

1. Avoid problems or solve them before they occur.

2. Reduce future family tension.

3. Strengthen the family with experience in coming to agreement.

4. Clarify your family's positions and reduce misunderstandings.

5. Help the family sort out its values and know what it stands for.

6. Improve future decisions by insuring that policy formation is informed and objective rather than made in the heat of battle.

7. Create more enthusiasm for and knowledge of the business.

8. Increase the likelihood of long-term business and family success, survival, and prosperity.

☛ **The policy-setting process strengthens and unifies the family.** Some families avoid creating policies because they fear the conflict that might occur as a result of addressing a sensitive issue. But **if a family can't handle conflict during a policy-setting process, imagine the conflict when the issues are live and real-time.** When family members work on creating policies, they learn to communicate with each other on difficult issues, solve problems together, address issues as a team, put their thinking together on paper, and resolve differences.

Even if the family were never to refer to the policies again (highly unlikely!), **the process of policy setting helps the family build skills, gain confidence, and increase its ability to face issues *as a family***. And because no family can ever anticipate every problem it will face or develop a policy on every issue it must deal with, the skills and confidence gained by developing policies can help it cope with unexpected issues.

Further, policies unify family members by helping them run in the same direction, not only now but in the future. We find that when families re-read certain policies together at family meetings, such as a code of conduct or a mission statement, it solidifies them as a family. It helps family members all understand what they have agreed to and brings them a little bit closer to one another.

☛ **Policies make things explicit**. As we said earlier in this booklet, families often set policy without intending to. Any decision that sets a precedent creates policy. But it is an *implied* policy. No one really talks about it or questions it openly. Family members just adhere to it because they think that's what's expected of them or because "that's the way we've always done it."

When family members go through the process of consciously creating policy and putting it in writing, however, they are making policy *explicit*. The process enables family members to question assumptions

The process of policy setting helps the family build skills, gain confidence, and increase its ability to face issues as a family.

and understand differing perspectives. And all can participate in making decisions about how they will govern themselves in the future.

When policies are not explicit, family members are free to interpret decisions any way they choose. The chances for misinterpretation, misleading information, and miscommunication increase. But if policies about how future decisions are to be made are fully discussed and laid out in advance, the family has a template from which to proceed. And chances are increased that family members will all be on the "same page."

Consider, for example, a family-owned moving company that has traditionally been open to any family member who wanted to join. Then competition stiffens. Controlling costs and productivity get renewed focus. The business simply cannot absorb more family members. Unaware of the current difficulties, Seretha, just about ready to graduate from college, announces her desire to join the company, like her older sister, Charlene, did five years before and her cousin, Reggie, did three years before that.

When her dad and uncle say they cannot take her on and suggest that she get some outside experience, Seretha is deeply hurt and angry. "Why does Charlene get to work in the company and I don't?" she asks her father. "I should have known she was your favorite."

Seretha now misinterprets the decision as one that means her father loves her less than he loves her sister, or possibly that he doesn't love her at all. How much better it would have been if the brothers had sat down long before their children were ready to come into the business and devised an employment policy that established criteria for family members entering the business. If they had created a clearly written document and shared it with their sons and daughters, Seretha would not now question her father's love. She would know that an open position in the company was one of the employment conditions (and that, of course, she would have to have the skills to fill the position). She would also understand that when things improved at the company, she would have a chance of joining it, just like her sister and cousin. The guidelines would be objective and explicit.

☛ **Family members become more educated on many levels.** Creating policies requires them to become even more knowledgeable about the business itself but also necessitates becoming familiar with and knowledgeable about the issues being discussed. Employment policies, for example, require investigation into employment practices. Compensation policies mean learning what compensation practices are being followed in the family's industry. Shareholder agreements call for educating yourself as a shareholder so that you can participate effectively in the discussion. In other words, when done right, the process of developing family business policies requires thought and homework.

Making policy also frequently calls for compromises that themselves offer opportunities for education. Sometimes, to find consensus, family members will exercise extraordinary creativity in searching for unique solutions that all can accept. The family may find that it has to bring in a consultant or facilitator to put the group through communications exercises so that family members can learn to talk to one another civilly about a difficult policy. These become skill-building endeavors. They enable family members to gain experience and success at handling problems together.

☛ **The family-business continuity-planning process is enhanced**. In the largest sense, policy development is about continuity planning — that is, how we prepare and educate the family to continue into the future as a business-owning family, as a successful family, as a healthy family, and as a strong family.

When a family creates policies, it is looking at all the elements that go into family-business continuity — the family's mission and vision, its values and beliefs, its principles and philosophies, its covenant or pledge (that is, what the family expects from the business and what the business has a right to expect from the family), and the business's strategy, culture, performance, and governance.

When family members work together to create policies, they discover what is important to them as a family and what is important to them as individuals. They gain major skills in communicating with one another effectively. They learn the art of compromise, in its finest sense. Creating policies helps the family sort out its values and know what it stands for.

> *When family members work together to create policies, they discover what is important to them as a family and what is important to them as individuals.*

III. *How To Develop Your Policies*

As you can see from reading Chapter 2, we urge families to put policies in place before the need arises. For example, consider a business run by a founder or founding partners with children still too young to join the company. It is easy to say, "I don't have to worry about the kids entering the business — that's still a few years off."

But if you want or hope or even fear the next generation's involvement, now is the time to develop an employment policy that sets forth the requirements and conditions under which offspring can join the family business. By high school, youngsters are beginning to think about their careers. A clear policy shared and discussed with them will help them make decisions about education and summer experiences.

A solid, well-communicated policy has the subtle capacity to guide decisions and interactions over the years with many potential positive outcomes.

It can help them prepare to make a real contribution to the business, avoiding the dangerous sense of entitlement that youngsters in a family business can develop. Finally, the policy can be put into practice when the young adult indicates a desire to join the business. **A solid, well-communicated policy has the subtle capacity to guide decisions and interactions over the years with many potential positive outcomes.** A policy on entering the business can focus the family's attention on a crucial issue that might otherwise be left to chance.

When developing your family business policy guide, focus not only on policies you need now. Looking ahead and anticipating what policies you need to put into place for the next generation is also critically important. A great strength of family businesses is long-term planning. Developing your policy guide is a place where that strength comes into play.

It is tempting to sit down and start making a list of policies that you think you need — and then go to work on writing policies. But, of course, it's not that simple. If you are a lone founder with younger children, you might be able to approach policy making that way — with some input from your spouse and some trusted advisors. Or, if

11

Factors That Influence Policy Development

■ Stage of the family business — first generation, second generation, and so on.

■ Size of the family, including how many family members work in the business or are shareholders.

■ Cultural background of the family — its ethnicity, religion, traditions, and values.

■ Culture of the business — including precedents that have already been set.

■ The family's openness or secretiveness.

■ The state of the family's harmony.

---

yours is a harmonious second- or third-generation business family with lots of experience and success at teamwork, this approach might work for you as well.

For most family businesses, however, things are more complex and the way policy development is approached depends upon a number of complicating factors, such as:

> *Policies must be customized to meet the needs of your particular family and your particular business. Each is unique.*

— the stage and size of the family and the business, including how many family members work in it or are shareholders.

— the harmony or lack of harmony in the family.

— the culture of the family — family values and practices will all affect how policies are shaped and the process a family goes through to reach agreement.

— the culture of the business, such as traditions that have already been developed or precedents already set.

Such complexities allow us to re-emphasize this important point: **Policies must be customized to meet the needs of your particular family and your particular business. Each is unique**. We would discourage you from taking any sample policy in this book or any policy used by another family business and adopting it wholesale without first going through the process that we lay out here. **Remember, as important as the content of the policies you adopt will be to your family and your business, the process that family members go through to agree on content is infinitely more valuable. Do not deprive your family of the opportunity to work together to develop the guidelines that may so importantly affect their lives and fortunes.**

> *Remember, as important as the content of the policies you adopt will be to your family and your business, the process that family members go through to agree on content is infinitely more valuable.*

EXHIBIT 3: ▇▇▇▇▇▇▇▇▇▇▇▇▇▇▇▇▇▇▇▇▇▇▇

Steps To Developing Family Business Policies

1. Determine whether your family is ready to start the process. Do they have the self-confidence, understanding, and family trust to begin?
2. Assign responsibilities (who will shepherd the process, lead discussion, be secretary, do research, etc.).
3. Identify issues the policy must address.
4. Seek advice and counsel from your board and/or advisors, other family members, and other family businesses.
5. Draft and discuss a preliminary policy.
6. Redraft the policy and get additional input from advisors.
7. Redraft and discuss again as needed.
8. Present committee's final draft to relevant family members.
9. Once the family has reached agreement, run the policy by your board and/or advisors for one last check.
10. Have the family ratify the policy.
11. Add the original policy and supporting documents to your master policy manual.

The Interlocking Pieces

The process of creating a family business policy guide, or even of creating just one policy to go into it, is not necessarily a linear one. In other words, we won't be describing Step One, Step Two, Step Three, and so on. When your family has some successful experience in policy-setting under its belt, you may be able to proceed in a step-by-step fashion that you have devised for yourselves. But until you arrive at that more ideal state, here are the essentials. Think of them as interlocking pieces, each one affecting or necessary to the other, like an intricate spider web (and perhaps equally delicate yet strong!).

1. Assessing the family and the business

Give considerable thought to describing your family and your business. It will help to put your thoughts down on paper, for your own review and for discussion with others later. As you record your description, make some notes about how what you see might affect the policies you select to develop or influence the development process itself. Here are some things to think about:

- **Size, composition, ownership and structure of the business.** Is the family business a small one still run by a founding entrepreneur or a founding partnership — two brothers, perhaps? If it's a second generation business, is it run by a single successor, two siblings, or five? Or is it a third- or fourth-generation business, with an ever-expanding number of family shareholders and family members working in the business? Does it have an active board of directors? Is the board made up of family members plus a few "inside" advisors (such as your lawyer or your non-family chief financial officer), or is it an "outside" board that includes key family executives plus several respected, independent business leaders?

- **Size of family and age of family members.** Is the chief executive nearing retirement, or still a relatively young entrepreneur? How old are the members of the next generation and how soon will they come knocking at the door of the business, asking to be let in? How many of them are there? Can the business absorb them all?

- **Characteristics of the family.** What are the family's shared goals and values? What are its hopes and dreams? What are its strengths (an excellent reputation in the community, for example)? Its weaknesses (a history of alcoholism, perhaps)? Does the family put the family before the business or the business before the family? Is it secretive or does it tend to communicate openly? How well does it tolerate differences among family members — for example, how does the family respond when Maria marries someone outside the family's faith or Aaron decides to become an actor instead of joining the family firm? Can children be treated differently or must they always be treated the same? What are its traditions? Is family leadership more likely to pass to the oldest male? To be shared among all the males in the next generation? To be shared among all the siblings in the next generation, regardless of gender? What are the roles of men and women in the family and the business? How is love expressed in the family? Does the family celebrate important events? What role does the family play in the community?

- **The state of family harmony.** Is the family harmonious or contentious? Have you put off developing policies because of the disagreements that you fear might result from the process? Or are family members able to handle discussion around difficult issues in a respectful, open manner? (A question for business leaders: Does the fear of family conflict lead you to unilaterally make family policy decisions without involving other family members in the process of policy development? If it does, you are likely to experience even greater conflict in the long run.)

EXHIBIT 4: ████████████████████████████████

Impediments to Policy Creation and Implementation

- Unresolved resentments in the family.
- Inadequate policy-development process.
- Lack of buy-in from family members.
- Low level of tolerance for differences among family members—some feel excluded.
- Poorly crafted language—too much room for misinterpretation.
- Out-of-date provisions.
- Unwillingness of family to enforce policy.
- Lack of policy on how to change policies.

2. Creating a decision-making environment

To create policies on which all can agree, most families may find that they must first create a good decision-making environment. By that, we mean an environment in which family members feel comfortable communicating openly with one another. They know they can express an idea without fear that someone else will jump all over it and them. They listen well and respectfully to one another. They don't pass judgment, but they are willing to challenge one another's ideas without getting personal and to be challenged without getting defensive. They don't misinterpret each other or assume they know one another's motivations. They aren't locked into a position. Instead, they are committed to working together toward solutions agreeable to all.

> *To create policies on which all can agree, most families may find that they must first create a good decision-making environment.*

EXHIBIT 5: ▬▬▬▬▬▬▬▬▬▬▬▬▬▬▬▬▬

Family Meeting Rules

"I" WILL —

- Listen to and respect alternative viewpoints.
- Deal professionally with family members.
- Avoid laying blame or making personal attacks.
- Not speak for others.
- Have regard for the needs and feelings of others.
- Take responsibility for my own emotions.
- Recognize my stress level and take responsibility for it.

"WE" WILL —

- Focus on our common vision.
- Have only one meeting.
- Encourage family members to speak out.
- Let others take responsibility for their own emotions.
- Recognize that conflict will occur and is okay.

In some families, however, various underlying issues get in the way of having a really good conversation about policies.

Sometimes, an individual family member lacks the ability to become a constructive part of the policy development process. For example, a family member who suffers from a severe lack of self-confidence will find being disagreed with very troubling. Such individuals require help in strengthening self-confidence before the process begins.

Individual goals can pose other problems. Marla and her brother, Kevin, for example, have their own hidden agendas — Marla has two sons in college and is hoping they someday will join the business her father started; Kevin thinks there's limited room for the next generation and is convinced his daughters are smarter. Kevin and Marla both attempt to manipulate the discussion about an employment policy so that the decision will benefit their own children, all the while talking about "the good of the business." Or Frank may be suspicious of the motives of his older brother, Fitz; he remembers how Fitz used to beat him up as a kid. It's hard for Frank to believe that Fitz really cares about his siblings now and has the good of the family and the business at heart.

An experienced, objective facilitator — a family business consultant or trusted, skilled advisor—can help to catalyze and guide the policy development process. Sometimes the family needs help in dealing with existing pains or issues so that sufficient trust can be restored to permit a fruitful policy discussion. **The greater the conflict in a family, the more it needs to work on figuring out what the family stands for and how it operates and then work on the easiest policies first.** That generally applies as well to families who are inexperienced in talking about the difficult issues that setting policy can present. Such families might begin by talking about the family's role in the community, focusing on philanthropy, for example, before working on potentially contentious issues like valuation formulas in a shareholder agreement.

By "practicing" on the easier policies first, a family gains experience in creating a decision-making environment. Once a decision-making environment is in place, policies flow from it more easily.

3. Involving everyone who needs to be involved

Provided they have sufficient maturity and understand enough about the business and the family, everyone in the family who's going to be affected by a policy should have an opportunity to make input and be involved in the discussion. When the younger generation is sufficiently mature and experienced, they should take the lead on developing policies. After all, they will be the ones who have to live with, abide by, and enforce those policies.

Some families will be ambivalent about having spouses present to hear or participate in the discussion. We realize that in some families, because of cultural background, spouses are never involved. Nevertheless, in our view, it's usually helpful at some point to involve the spouses, because they need to understand and agree with the policies developed. Family business policies will impact their children and their security, whether or not they work in the business or own its stock.

Even though a small committee may be assigned to draft a policy, the whole family should have an opportunity to discuss the draft and send it back for redraft until agreement is reached. Ultimately, involvement supports the implementation of policy. If individuals affected by a policy aren't brought into the development process and don't feel they have "bought into" it, they may feel little or no obligation to live by it.

4. Deciding how to decide

The process of developing policy will be somewhat different for smaller families (say, 4 to 12 people involved) than for medium-sized families (12-20 people) or larger families. In fact, deciding how to decide may be your family's first policy decision!

EXHIBIT 6: ▮▮▮▮▮▮▮▮▮▮▮▮▮▮▮▮▮▮▮▮▮▮▮▮▮▮▮▮▮▮▮▮

Start with the Easier Policies

EASIER	HARDER	HARDEST
Employment (When not facing it anytime soon)	Compensation	Governance (Family Council and Board of Directors)
Code of Conduct	Publicity	Shareholder Agreement
Philanthropy	Dividends	Conflict of Interest

When families are inexperienced at developing policies or there is considerable disharmony among family members, build skills in working together by beginning with the easier policies. Developing policy will be difficult for any issue about which overt conflict already exists. Exhibit 6 lists examples of levels of difficulty.

☞ **Smaller families** may choose to operate as a committee-of-the-whole. A facilitator or moderator or "shepherd" would be chosen — that is, someone to move the process and discussion along. This can be a professional facilitator from outside the family, a competent and trusted family advisor, or a family member skilled at keeping things moving. Some families may want to have one member oversee the process but have someone else lead the discussion. Most likely, the smaller family will decide on policy by consensus. (Keep in mind that "smaller family" does not necessarily mean a small business. It just refers to the number of relevant family members involved.) If your family handles the process this way, we recommend separating the roles of meeting chair/facilitator, agenda setter, and meeting logistics coordinator. This spreads both the burden and the involvement among several people.

☞**Medium-sized families** may break up into sub-committees or task forces, each assigned to a particular policy. One task force might be assigned to draft a policy on marriage contracts, for example. When it's ready with its first draft, it would bring the draft back to the family, which would discuss it as a committee-of-the-whole. The medium-sized family, like the smaller family, could reach agreement by consensus.

☞**Larger families** require more formal decision-making or governance structures. A large family may have a family council, a subset of the family that serves as its leadership or governance body. The whole family could be regarded as the "family assembly." In a large family, the family council could initiate and draft policy statements. After seeking input and circulating the draft to family members, the council could put the draft to the family assembly for a vote. Since unanimity is unlikely in a large family, it's desirable that the family has already made some decisions about how it will decide—such as "majority rules" or "75 percent rules." In the largest families, the family council may be entrusted with the power to adopt policy without the vote of the entire family.

5. Initiating policy

Policy can be initiated in one of several ways. And it's not just a matter of *who* initiates it but *where* it is initiated. One of the struggles that family businesses face in relation to given issues is, "Should the business be making the policy or should the family be making the policy?" We find it varies from family to family, but still, it's the family who decides where policy will be made.

For example, a family may decide that compensation will be determined within the business by senior management and be based on market rates. That policy sends a message to family members saying nephews can't get paid on the basis of being in the family, or mothers can't interfere in the business and say, "My son deserves as much as your son does because he's a family member."

A family may also decide that the next CEO is going to be chosen by the board of directors based strictly on business criteria, whether the candidate is a family member or not. Another family might mandate that CEOs should be family members and direct the board to do everything possible within good business practice to assure that the next CEO is a family member.

It's important to note that when policy is made within the business, people outside the family — key non-family executives and non-family board members — often become involved in the initiating process. For example, non-family managers charged with supervising young family employees eagerly seek guidance on how to do that sensitive job. A policy statement on the subject can be very helpful to the supervisor, the employee and a non-employed parent or spouse who hears about a performance appraisal that focused on opportunities for improvement.

Another question is what generation will initiate policy? As we have indicated, sometimes the first generation, as it makes decisions that harden into precedents, is creating policy without even realizing it. Subsequent generations may follow the precedents, perhaps without realizing they're accepting policy. One of the exercises you might find useful is to attempt to identify implicit policies that exist in your family and business. Family members could begin to write them down and, through discussion, determine whether they still serve the family and the business well or need to be modified. In this way, the family can consciously and thoughtfully make old, implicit policies explicit or replace them if they are no longer viable.

We encourage an interactive process between the generations. As an example, the first generation might ask the second generation to start answering a series of questions, such as, "When you get into this kind of situation, what will guide you? What will your policy be?" Members of the second generation can get together, work up their policy, and present their solution to the first generation. The first generation, may say, "This is great!" or "I'm a little uncomfortable with this. Do you really think this is going to work?" The two generations can exchange ideas until finally, the first generation says, "The ball's in your court. You make the rules." The second generation then "makes the rules" until it initiates a similar process with the third generation.

6. Separating the past from the future

One of the major challenges families have in setting policy when the next generation comes along is separating the past from the future. Let's say a family business started by two brothers and still run by them is trying to develop an employment policy. The brothers have seven children between them—three in the business, two in college, and two in high school. The three in the business, with the encouragement of some outside advisors, are pushing for a requirement that family members have a college degree before they enter the business. But their fathers are saying, "*We* didn't have a college education and look how great this business is. It was good enough for us. Why isn't it good enough for you?"

It's hard, of course, to argue with the fathers' success. But it's important for the senior generation — for *all* generations — to think of policy as being about the future, not the past. In this case, the family needs to discuss how the future will differ for the business and what the business will need to continue to succeed.

The same can be said for old resentments and conflicts that still create ill feeling in the present. In some cases, families seek professional help to deal with them. Other families make the decision to act as though "the past is the past. Let's go forward."

Precedents are also a part of the past. Emily, who owns a significant amount of stock in the family business, may say, "My mother had a seat on the board and I want to have a seat on the board." She doesn't work in the business and being on the board would be her only direct connection to it. But other family members, particularly those who work in the company, see the need to move toward a board with a majority of talented outsiders. If Emily is on the board, she takes the seat of one of those outsiders. The family needs to develop a policy concerning membership on the board of directors and other policies responsive to Emily's and other family members' needs to feel connected to their family business.

"Mother was on the board, so I should be too," has probably lost its value as a guide to family business decisions.

Each new generation in a family business creates a new set of dynamics and a new set of issues about which policy must be made.

Each new generation in a family business creates a new set of dynamics and a new set of issues about which policy must be made. If they're thoughtful about it, family members—old and young—will say, "The way we did things in the past isn't necessarily going to be sufficient for how we need to do things in the future. We have to think about that and make some new decisions."

EXHIBIT 7:

Eight Keys To Successful Policy Making

1. Create a decision-making environment — one where family members are willing and wanting to communicate openly with one another.

2. Involve everyone who needs to be involved.

3. Focus on the needs of the future; let go of the past.

4. Get outside input — from advisors, independent board members, other successful family businesses.

5. Don't get "frozen into position." Keep an open mind and hear all points of view.

6. Look at the big picture of what's best for the whole family and for the business; avoid thinking only in terms of self-interest.

7. Let policies grow out of the values, beliefs, philosophies, and principles of the family.

8. Decide in advance how policies will be approved and enacted.

The "Core" Process

Within the context of all that has been outlined above, we list below some of the individual steps you and your family can expect to go through in developing a policy for your policy guide.

We urge families to hold off discussion or debate of any policy until after step "e." When discussion begins too early in the process, family members start to "freeze up" in their opinions and get locked into positions, often based on some self-interest. This is natural — parents in a family business probably hope their children will join the company or become shareholders; each sibling or cousin in the next generation may aspire to be CEO. What's important in policy development is that family members set aside individual interests as best they can, and consider the best interests of the business and the family. These steps are designed to help family members avoid getting frozen so that they can move forward toward adopting policies that best fit the needs of the family and the business:

a. **Choose a policy to begin developing.** Remember the factors that go into this choice: (1) Policy guidelines you need now and in the next generation; (2) The stage of your family's business—first generation, second, third, and so on; (3) Your family's experience in developing policy—the less experienced you are, the more you need to start with a simpler policy; (4) The level of harmony in your family—again, the more conflicted family members are, the more they need to start with a simpler policy on which they can "practice" and gain experience in working together.

b. **Assign roles and responsibilities.** You'll need someone to shepherd the process and perhaps a separate person to lead discussion; someone to record the discussion; several people (or perhaps the entire committee or task force) to do research; someone to write the first draft and revisions; and, ultimately, someone to gather policies and background documents (data gathered, notes on discussion, etc.) in a master policy manual—a large notebook, perhaps.

c. **Be sure the family has established meeting rules.** Some key rules include: How will decisions be made? What happens if someone is not participating in the discussion? How will discussion

23

be managed? (See *Family Meetings: How to Build A Successful Family and a Stronger Business,* No. 2 in the Family Business Leadership Series.)

d. **Begin to identify the dimensions of the policy.** For example, some of the considerations related to an employment policy might be: Should in-laws be eligible to work in the business? If somebody leaves the business, can they come back? Can a mother with young children work part-time—indefinitely? If somebody has been fired, can he come back? (This booklet offers help on roughing out the dimensions of a number of different policies in Chapters 4, 5 and 6.)

e. **Seek advice and counsel outside the family.** Read policies that other family businesses have adopted. Visit with other families and interview them, asking such questions as: What has your experience been? What lessons have you learned? What kinds of things have you thought about? What mistakes have you made? Get the advice of your family business advisors—your lawyer, your accountant, the independent directors on your board.

f. **Draft and discuss a preliminary policy statement.** The draft should begin with a short statement, or preamble, describing the philosophy behind each policy. For example, a dividend policy would not begin with the formula the family would use to determine dividends; it would begin with a statement of what the family hopes to accomplish and what values it wishes to express with its dividend policy.

Agreement on the decision-making process is more important than agreement on the policy itself.

Remember to have someone capture the discussion on paper—that will be invaluable to you in reviewing what you've done and avoiding misinterpretation. It will also be invaluable to future generations, helping them to understand why you've made the choices you've made and the struggle that went into your choices, including the differing and sometimes dissenting points of view of particular family members.

g. **Ask your board or outside advisors to review the draft and give input.** Have you covered all the issues? Is it fair?

24

h. Redraft and re-discuss the policy as needed. Date each draft so that you have a recorded history of the policy. Continue to have someone record the discussions.

i. Once the drafting committee has reached agreement, the document can be presented for a final decision to the appropriate body, be it the relevant members of a smaller family or medium-sized family, or the family council of a larger family.

j. Once the family or family council has reached agreement, the policy is ready to be ratified. But wait. We suggest you not ratify a policy at the same meeting at which you've come to agreement. Run it by the board of directors or outside advisors one more time, saying, "These are the family's final feelings on this policy. If you see anything glaringly wrong, please let us know. Otherwise, this is our opinion on the subject."

k. Assuming board members or outside advisors don't see a problem, go ahead and ratify the policy. A nice touch is to pass the final document around and have all relevant members of the family sign it.

l. Add the original policy, with its supporting documents, to your master policy manual.

Remember: perceived justice results mostly from the process being perceived as just. Agreement on the decision-making process is more important than agreement on the policy itself.

Avoiding Problems

Occasionally, somebody—most likely a parent—comes up with a set of policies and tries to impose them on the family. One typical response is to buy into them and say, "Dad came up with them. Fine. We'll go with them." Another is to say, "These are terrible. I can't believe you did this." The problem with the first response is that family members affected by the policies had no voice in the policies and the policies may not, in fact, be "fine." The problem with the second response is that it cuts off discussion and creates resentment. "I've worked so hard and now you're disrespecting me," the father may say.

When a parent tries to impose policies, one response is for the children to come up with their own alternative set of policies. This, of course, requires the children to be unified. Sometimes, Dad comes up with a set of policies *because* the children are not unified, in hopes of unifying them. Unfortunately, such action usually creates further dissension.

Another problem families run into is misinterpretation of a policy. No matter how carefully written, language is always subject to misinterpretation. (Consider how much we still argue over the Constitution of the United States.) One of the reasons we recommend recording the rationale for a policy is that it helps family members to understand its intent when questions are raised.

The development of policy is an ongoing, evolutionary, almost perpetual process. The creation of a policy can take many meetings, over months or even years. Many revisions are sometimes needed before a final draft is approved.

In any family, policies need to be revisited and reviewed periodically to be sure they meet the needs of the family and the business, and to be updated if they do not. **In larger family businesses, a standing committee of the family council may meet once a year or more often to review policies and to arrange for redrafting as necessary.** Some families even place sunset laws on their policies. Basically, they say, "These policies are for this generation. The next generation should develop its own. Until they do, they can use these as help or as models." No policy guide is complete without a policy on reviewing and amending policies.

> *Policies should emerge from the family's values, beliefs, philosophies and principles.*

Policy-setting requires creativity and, in its noblest form, the art of compromise. **Ideally, however, policies are not a compromise of personal opinions—yours versus mine. Policies should emerge from the family's values, beliefs, philosophies and principles.** Families who have laid a foundation by having discussed and defined their values and beliefs and developed written values or mission statements will be ahead of the game when it comes to developing such specific policies as shareholder agreements, dividend policies, and marriage contracts. Members of such families are less likely to think only in terms of their own perspectives and to approach policy from a larger perspective, asking such questions as: What are we trying to accomplish? What do we stand for? What do we believe in? What's important for the future?

26

Policy-making comes more easily to families who know what they stand for, and such families are more likely to make policy development an effective part of their continuity-planning process.

IV. What Policies Do You Need? And When?

While there are no hard and fast rules about what policies a family firm needs or when it needs them, we believe there are core policies that benefit most, if not all, business-owning families. These include:

- Family decision making/governance policies
- Compensation/performance evaluation policies
- Employment policies
- Codes of conduct

Shareholder agreements could be added to this list. However, a shareholder agreement is more than just one policy. It is, in fact, a legal document that encompasses a number of policies related to ownership issues. You will find shareholder agreements treated separately in Chapter 5.

As a family becomes larger and more complex, its need for policies increases and the dynamics surrounding the issues that these policies address change. For example, in a first-generation business, a founding entrepreneur may be the sole decision maker or may make decisions in concert with a spouse. In the second generation, group decision making involves two generations, adult siblings and, initially, their parent-founders. Third generation decision making may involve siblings, cousins, parents, aunts and uncles, in-laws, and grandparents. Each new stage of a family business requires renewed thoughtfulness about family business policies.

Again, you will want to examine precedents to understand how they affect present and future success. For example, in one business we know, the two brothers paid themselves equally and established a tradition of equal payment among family employees. For them,

As a family becomes larger and more complex, its need for policies increases and the dynamics surrounding the issues that these policies address change.

equal pay meant "we own the business equally and we all care about each other equally." The compensation policy also was a way to express the value of "one for all and all for one."

The policy worked reasonably well in the second generation,

when five of the founders' children worked in the business. But by the third generation, when 14 family members and several in-laws worked in the company, the tradition had become a detriment. Many family members were overpaid (and a few were not paid enough). Non-family employees were resentful of the favoritism they saw shown to family members. While conflict escalated, the family could not find a way to revise a policy that no longer worked. An angry family was distracted and unable to effectively operate their business.

In this chapter, we will introduce you to the purposes behind these core policies and suggest the issues—some of them difficult and emotional—that each policy raises for a family. These issues need thorough discussion by family members as they set out to develop their own policies. We will also provide guidelines for when a family might begin putting these policies in place.

In Chapter 6, we look at a host of other policies a family might want to consider—some of which a family, depending on its own circumstances, might find just as important as the core policies outlined here.

Family Decision Making/Governance

Essentially, governance refers to how family-business decisions are made. Before a family begins to address development of any other policies, it may need to address how it makes decisions—simply because it's hard to move forward on policies until you agree on how you're going to agree.

In the first generation, family members may come together in a somewhat informal fashion and make decisions together. When members of the second generation come into the business, they may form a sibling partnership. (See *Making Sibling Teams Work: The Next Generation*, No.10 in The Family Business Leadership Series). When the family gets to the third or fourth generation and the family has expanded in size, governance may involve a family council, a board of directors, and various board and family committees and subcommittees that include family members inside and outside of the business. *Family Business Governance: Maximizing Family and Business Potential*, No. 8 in the Family Business Leadership Series, deals with boards, family councils and governance, and discusses the many policies families should consider in this area.

It's hard to move forward on policies until you agree on how you're going to agree.

Family Decision Making

☞ How do we make decisions as a family? By consensus? By vote? We've found that families who can use voting and live comfortably with votes seem to have greater family harmony and business prosperity in the long run.

☞ If we make decisions by voting, who is eligible to vote? Do we vote based on the number of shares held or is it one person, one vote? Do in-laws have a right to vote (some families even struggle with whether same-sex significant others should be invited to participate)? How old must the kids be before they get the right to vote?

☞ Do we follow Robert's Rules? Do we need a quorum? Does a simple majority rule?

☞ Are there issues we vote on and issues we decide by consensus?

☞ If we reach a stalemate, how do we resolve it? For example, do we turn to a third party?

☞ When do members of the senior generation stop participating in the vote?

☞ Can family members vote by proxy? Or through other people?

Board of Directors

☞ Does the family want a legal board of directors or a more informal advisory board?

☞ What are the rights of family members to be on the company board of directors? What family members should be on the board and how are they selected? Will family members be rotated so that every one gets a turn? What balance does the family want in terms of family members versus non-family members on the board?

☞ What are the criteria for family members serving on the board? For non-family members? How are family members prepared for service on the board? How are they educated about the role of the board in a business?

☞ Do family members get paid for being on the board? (In many families, family members who are employees do not get a fee for sitting on the board, but family members who are not employed in the business receive the same fee that an independent director would get. In other families, no family members get paid to be on the board whether or not they work in the business. And in still others, every family member on the board is paid a fee.)

☛ Who should chair the board and how is the chair selected? What is the role of the chair?

☛ Can family members who are not board members sit in on board meetings as observers? Can in-laws? If board meetings are open, how can attendance be kept to a manageable number? And should there be a closed session of the board, where all visitors are excused?

What are the criteria for family members serving on the board?

☛ Should family members not on the board have the opportunity to contact independent directors on their own?

☛ Should we draw up a code of conduct for family board members—for example, reminding them that their role is to ask strategic questions, not inquire about operational details? (In some families, the matter of whether or not a family member can do needlework during board meetings actually becomes a big issue!)

☛ How long will a term on the board be? How often will the board meet? Will members be paid expenses for attending?

☛ What committees need to be established and who will serve on them?

Family Councils

The creation of a family council to handle family decision making raises questions very similar to those above. In addition, the family will want to give thought to such questions as:

☛ Should the family council be used to give family members not in the business a larger role?

☛ What is the role of the family council in relationship to the board of directors? How will the two bodies communicate with each other?

☛ What are the family council's responsibilities to the family? For example, will it help educate family members about the business? Will it provide a mechanism for family members to have fun together?

Compensation/Performance Evaluation

Compensation is an area around which jealousies and resentments can easily build. Pay conveys messages about value, and offers freedom and security. Few other issues can become as emotionally charged. The value of compensation and performance evaluation policies is that they make explicit—to family members active in the business and to those who are not—what the family's agreed-upon policies are regarding all forms of compensation. They also set forth performance expectations, so that there should be no surprises when family member employees who fall short must pay a penalty. They help a family meet a goal of being objective and fair about matters of compensation and performance evaluation as they affect family members. A family should have compensation and performance evaluation policies in place by the time members of the second generation begin to enter the business.

As a family business evolves, going from first generation to second and third, the matter of compensation and performance tends to move from family-based policy toward decisions made within the business. But even the fact that the decision-making process moves into the business arena is a reflection of a decision by the family that compensation decisions are to be made in the business and not by the family.

Compensation and performance evaluation policies help a family to be objective and fair about these matters.

Like the topic of governance, the consideration of compensation and performance evaluation is so important to a family business that the Family Business Leadership Series devotes a whole booklet to it — see Family Business Leadership Series No. 5, *Family Business Compensation.*

For the purposes of this discussion, however, the key issues that families will be exploring are:

☛ What is our philosophy on compensation as it relates to market compensation? Do we favor paying market rates or is it our view that family employees get special treatment? If we pay everyone equally now and it works because we are still a small family, can we be open to changing that policy as the family grows?

☛ Should compensation be an "open book" in our family? In other words, will we share information on compensation of family members with each other?

☛ Will we use independent sources to help validate our compensation decisions, such as consultants, independent board members, or trade associations?

☛ What is our philosophy on perks and expense accounts for family members? For non-family members?

☛ To attract and keep talented family employees, shall family members get stock options as a part of their bonus? If so, how will this eventually affect voting power? Are we prepared for the possibility that some family members would start to accumulate more stock than other family members?

☛ How do we relate performance to compensation? How will we determine standards of performance and who will determine those standards? What rewards do we offer for exceptional performance? What penalties when performance does not meet expectations?

☛ How will any of our decisions regarding compensation and performance affect non-family employees? Will they feel that they are treated fairly? Will our policy be known to non-family employees? Will our policies motivate or demotivate them? Will their perception be that family members get special treatment?

☛ What about family employees who devote a great deal of office time to public service? How does the family value that and compensate for it? In what ways does public service benefit the company and the family?

☛ How will our compensation decisions affect the profitability and success of our business? Our ability to compete? Do they make good business sense?

The same questions should be asked to establish policy about perquisites (perks). For many families, unclear rationale for or undisclosed perks cause as many problems as compensation.

Employment

At some point, a family needs to determine under what rules family members can participate as employees in the family business. Founders will probably want to start considering this question before their children reach high school so that they can adequately communicate expectations to the children by the time they reach the career-planning stage. In fact, this issue is the one that often initiates thinking about family business policies. If policies about employment of family members are thought out well in advance, the exercise can set a positive tone for developing future policies. If the discussion occurs only when disagreement erupts over a job offer, policy making will never be smooth. Members of the second generation will want to review any existing policy and modify it to meet the needs of a growing family and growing business that will mark the third generation, and so on.

Here are some of the dimensions of employment policies—sometimes called participation policies—for family members to consider:

☛ What is the history of family members' participation in the family business? Are previous policies and precedents still useful?

☛ Will family members be permitted to work in the business? (Some families ban them altogether, fearing that the business will not select the best candidates for employment or leadership because of biases toward family members. Other families believe it's important to have family members employed in and leading the business to represent and instill the values of the family.)

☛ Does the family favor a "blue-sky" policy—that is, a policy that promises a job in the family business for every family member who wants one? Or will family members be hired only if positions are open and family members are qualified to fill them?

☛ What process will we use to hire people, including family members? Who makes the decision to hire? What criteria will be used? Will family members be favored over non-family? Will family members be required to fill out an application and go through the human resources department, just like any other applicant?

☛ What qualifications must family members meet? What educational requirements, for example? What outside work experience? (Families are often divided on the issue of outside work experience, with some members favoring it and others saying, "We didn't have outside experience and we did just fine. Why should we make our children work elsewhere first? They can get great experience here.") To what extent does education count for outside experience? If Stacia goes to law school, for example, does that count toward her outside work experience? What quality of job will be considered as outside experience? If Tol is a clerk at a local supermarket, does that count?

☛ Will only those family members who have the potential to rise to top management be permitted to join the business? Or is it perfectly fine to have some family members as production-line workers, foremen, or truck drivers, as long as they understand that that's as far as they can go?

☛ Will in-laws be permitted to work in the family business? What about ex-spouses of family members?

☛ Should we have a family employment committee that continues to address issues of family employment? What non-family members, if any, should be included on the committee? (Some families find that non-family members, provided they have affection for the family, can keep family members from fighting with one another over employment issues. They can help family members avoid situations where one family committee member says to another: "I made the decision in favor of your child last time. It's your turn to make the decision in favor of my child now.")

☛ How can family members (and other employees) move up in the company?

☛ How do we terminate a family member who's not performing? What steps should we go through before someone is finally let go? (Some families are quick and final; others, as we usually recommend, provide a period for cooling off, reflection, and hopefully change, before making the final decision to terminate.)

☛ If a family member leaves the business voluntarily, can he or she come back? If a family member has been fired, can he or she come back?

☛ What about full-time versus part-time employment? For example, can a mother with young children work part-time indefinitely if she's a family member?

☛ What about internships or summer employment or part-time jobs for younger family members?

☛ By what age should a family member commit to the family business? (To maintain harmony and teamwork, some families stipulate that family members must join the business by the time they are 35. Such families don't want family members wandering back when they're 48 and in search of a job.)

A footnote about educational requirements and outside work experience: From what we have observed, a business does not always demand the benefits of outside work experience or higher levels of education. The benefits really depend on the business's need and the family member's acumen and abilities. Nevertheless, there *are* benefits to the individual: A family member can gain greater self-confidence and self-worth by knowing he or she can succeed outside the family business. And the time it takes members of the younger generation to gain advanced degrees or outside work experience may provide the senior generation with more time to assess potential next-generation candidates for leadership and come up with a succession program. What families need to guard against, however, is requiring advanced degrees and outside experience as a means of circumventing succession conflicts rather than dealing with succession head on.

Codes of Conduct

Family codes of conduct usually address two issues: How family members treat one another, and how family members conduct themselves with the world outside the family. Because codes of conduct address behavior, families may find they need to grapple with family members' concerns over personal freedom especially when they are developing an external code of conduct. The question is, "What happens if 'being myself' conflicts with what the group wants?"

Among the issues that arise in the development of codes of conduct are:

How We Treat Each Other

☛ What rules will we follow with respect to what we say about each other to our spouses? To parents? Can we agree not to badmouth each other to other family members or to employees?

☞ How will we handle conflict with one another? Can we make a pact to solve our problems with each other directly and not involve other family members? Can we commit ourselves to an attitude of discussion as opposed to argument? Can we adopt secret codes or signals by which we let another family member know we're in trouble and need him or her to be concerned about our psychological safety. The code words chosen can mean: "You're getting under my skin and I'm losing my cool. Cease and desist. Give me some time and space. I'm about to come unraveled."

☞ How do we support each other?

☞ Can we solve our problems behind closed doors and not air them in front of employees?

☞ What information should we share with one another? For example, can we share estate planning information that's relevant to the business and to one another?

☞ How shall we communicate with one another? Should we have a communications policy?

☞ Should family members who don't work in the business be allowed to contact employees? For example, can your brother Charlie, an artist, feel free to call the chief financial officer and grill him about the latest financial reports?

How We Conduct Ourselves with the Outside World

☞ What should be our stance with regard to confidentiality about the business and the family?

☞ How shall we handle media relations? Can anyone in the family speak to the media, or shall we designate one person? Do we want to seek publicity for the business? For the family? Or do we prefer to be "low-profile"? How will we handle it when one family member seems to attract all the limelight?

☞ Do we encourage involvement in civic affairs, politics, or other organizations on the part of family members? If so, how much or how little? Is there a limit? What if a family member wants to participate in an organization that is controversial—the National Rifle

Association or the Sierra Club, for example?

☛ What work habits do we expect from each other? Are there work rules we want to adopt for ourselves? A standard of dress for the workplace?

☛ Should family members be allowed to date employees?

☛ What about our lifestyles? Is it respected if one family member drives a fancy car, owns in a lavish house, and lives flamboyantly, totally out of sync with other family members, who are understated and want to play down family wealth?

The four core policies described in this chapter, plus a shareholder agreement described in the next, will provide a firm foundation for a family and its business. Going through the process of developing these documents will strengthen and unite the family; having them in place will help assure peak performance from the business and enable it — and the family — to weather future difficulties.

V. Shareholder Agreements

Because it contains several family business policies, developing a shareholder agreement is often a great challenge to business-owning families. Such an agreement is needed whenever a business has more than one owner (as in a partnership), or when a founder begins to distribute shares to children or other family members. Shareholder agreements — sometimes called "ownership agreements" or "buy-sell agreements" — cover a host of issues, setting forth who gets to own stock, who gets to vote their stock, how and when stock is transferred, and the terms and conditions under which it may be bought and sold. **Drawn properly, shareholder agreements protect the business by keeping it in control of those most able to lead it. They also protect the family's interest in the business by preventing shares from falling into the hands of individuals outside the family. Drawn up improperly, they can create family problems and business problems.**

Ultimately, a shareholder agreement is a contract put into final form for a family by an attorney. But note that we say "final form." **We believe it's absolutely essential for family members to develop the initial draft of a shareholder agreement, thoughtfully considering the questions set forth below.** Attorneys may be very helpful in the process, but too often they have set ideas about what makes a good shareholder agreement. They approach the task of preparing one with a different perspective than family members do. Attorneys may have biases regarding ownership dilution, the use of insurance, or ideas about in-laws and ownership. Too often, attorneys use standardized shareholder agreements that are unlikely to be responsive to the particular needs, values, and goals of your family and your business.

Another danger of assigning an attorney to draft the agreement is that family members are then tempted to talk about the draft that the attorney has prepared rather than discuss the fundamental questions they need to address. So, instead of the family massaging an attorney's draft, we recommend that the family write its own and then let the attorney shape the family's wishes into a legal document. Tell

Drawn properly, shareholder agreements protect the business by keeping it in control of those most able to lead.

41

the attorney, "This is what we are trying to accomplish." When you do that, it means family members have given a lot of thought to and engaged in a lot of interaction about what they want in the document, have arrived at a point where they can articulate to a lawyer what they have agreed upon, and, as a result, can help the attorney help them achieve their own goals. In other words, the family needs to stay in charge of the end result.

As your family discusses the questions related to shareholder agreements, expect emotional issues to surface. How a family handles some of these issues can be equated with how it expresses love — for example, parents who decide to distribute stock equally among their children may be trying to convey that they love all of their children equally. Families trying to determine when individual family members may sell stock back to the company will come face to face with their attitudes about family members' ability to have cash in their pockets or their freedom to leave the company. Some family members may worry that when others sell stock and come into cash, they will spend it foolishly. Still others may hold to the view that only family members working in the company should be entitled to ownership in it. Here are some of the questions family members will want to think about as they develop a shareholder agreement. They are divided between the two basic issues of (1) who can own shares and (2) how shares can be transferred by gift, sale or bequest.

Who Can Own Shares?

■ How many can own? (This question is particularly important for S corporations, which are limited by law to 75 shareholders, and in considering how widespread distribution of stock can affect the business.)

■ Must family members meet certain requirements to be owners? For example, is ownership limited to those who have attained certain educational levels, or those who participate regularly in family council meetings? Must a family member be working in the business or have declared an intention to work in the business by a certain age to qualify for business ownership? (The answers to such questions will depend on family values and goals as well as on whether family members are provided education and motivation to be good shareholders. In some families, those family members who have met agreed-upon requirements get

42

voting stock while the rest have non-voting stock convertible to voting stock once the requirements are met.)

- Should stock have different voting rights — that is, should there be voting stock and nonvoting stock? (Some families use this device to enable certain family members to retain control of fundamental business decisions.)

- Can in-laws be owners?

- Can non-family employees own stock? If so, should ownership be limited to certain executives or be available to all employees, perhaps through an employee stock ownership plan (ESOP)?

- What happens as the family grows larger? Will one branch of the family own more stock and have more control? Should we attempt to equalize ownership among branches? (When a founder, for example, gives controlling interest to a son who has assumed leadership of the business, branches of the family in succeeding generations may be sensitive to the disparity of ownership. Resentment may build in the "have not" branches unless a family decides to address the issue.)

- What is the base percentage that the CEO/Chair should own?

- What is the base percentage that the family as a whole should own?

- Can a trust hold stock for the benefit of family or others?

How and When Is Stock Given, Bought, and Sold?

- Under what circumstances does the company have the right to buy stock back? Under what circumstances is it obligated to do so? (If an owner dies, for example, do the remaining owners have the right to buy the deceased owner's interest? If an owner becomes permanently disabled, can the others purchase his shares or may he continue to be an owner even though he can no longer work in the business?)

- Is there a maximum dollar or percentage amount the company will buy back in a given year?

- How will buyouts be funded? Should life insurance be put in place to meet the cost of a deceased owner's shares so that the company doesn't have to come up with the money? Should the company set aside a certain dollar amount every year to meet its maximum repurchase obligation for that year?

- Under what circumstances do family members have the right to sell their stock? Or, are there any rights to sell? May shareholders sell at any time, or only at specific ages and/or intervals? (For example, no right to sell at all until age 25, then at 35, 45, 55, 65, and any time at all thereafter. Or, perhaps, once a year or every 10 years after the adoption of the agreement.)

- When an owner wants to sell, does the company and then do the other owners have the right of first refusal to buy the shares before they are sold to an outside party? (We caution families not to design the shareholder agreement to lean too heavily on the desire to save taxes. We know of at least one agreement where the company had first obligation to buy stock, which is an effective estate-tax technique if the company is buying stock from members of the older generation. In this case, however, when a young family member died and the company had to purchase the stock, the older generation's taxable estate was actually increased.)

- If an owner wants to sell, what percentage of his shares must he sell? Some family businesses live by the rule, "sell all or nothing."

- If an owner wants to sell, how quickly must she notify the others? How fast can she get her money out? How will her shares be valued? Are her shares subject to a minority discount and, if so, can she negotiate a higher price? If money will be paid out over time, what interest rate, if any, will be paid and what will the time period be?

- What if the business can't afford to redeem the shares of an owner who wants to liquidate?

- Do family members have a right — or perhaps an obligation — to buy out shares that are about to be distributed to an owner's spouse during divorce proceedings?

- If an owner holds both voting and nonvoting stock and wants to redeem some of the shares, must he proportionately redeem some of the voting stock and nonvoting stock?

- Should the terms of a buy back be subject to the board of directors' determination of the company's ability to pay?

- How will the company be valued? By a formula or a routine appraisal? Who will share in the information?

- Can family members make investments in the company and buy stock from it? If so, how much can they purchase? We have seen some families allow such purchases up to the point where the family branches become equalized in ownership.

A shareholder agreement is one of the most difficult, most complex documents that a family can develop. As your family undertakes the work of creating one of its own, pay special attention to learning as much as you can about shareholder agreements. You may want to bring in an outside resource person — not necessarily a lawyer — to help you think through what you want to do. You'll find it helpful to review shareholder agreements of other family businesses as well and to visit with leaders of other family businesses to learn about the rationales that went into their documents. Once your family has come to agreement on what it wants, then instruct the attorney on how to construct your family's shareholder agreement.

VI. *Other Policies to Consider*

In addition to the core policies that will benefit most family businesses, there are a number of other issues around which a particular family may find it helpful to develop policies.

Some of the possibilities are listed below. Again, we outline a few of the dimensions of each topic and the issues that each raises for a family. We give special attention to conflict of interest and philanthropy policies because they are especially intriguing and they raise so many fundamental questions for business-owning families to consider.

Conflict of Interest and Self-Dealing

The fundamental question that needs to be explored and decided is: Can family members do business with the business? For example, your son is an architect. Should he be hired to design the family firm's new cafeteria? Or, you don't work in the family business but you're a shareholder; you're also a licensed pilot and you own your own airplane. Should your brother, who runs the company, hire you to fly executives between company plants in different states?

We frequently see business families encouraging such relationships. However, many problems can arise. A family can benefit from consciously developing policy around conflict of interest and self-dealing, discussing such questions as: If we use family members as suppliers, how do we establish pay? How do we evaluate their performance? Where do we draw the line? Are we sending a message that any family member can do business with the family firm, no matter what their business is?

An important issue is perception. Even if you can arrange arm's-length deals with family members and objectively evaluate their performance, what signal will you be sending to family business employees? Despite your best efforts, and despite employees' willingness to give owner-managers of healthy businesses significant degrees of latitude, will they think family members are just feathering their own nests?

What precedents will you be setting? If family members are allowed to do certain things, are non-family employees also permitted to do them? If the VP-sale's wife is starting a meeting-planning service, would the family be comfortable having her plan its next sales meeting?

Conflict-of-interest policies also include the dimension of investments. Can family members invest in suppliers to our family business? If I learn about a fantastic real estate investment opportunity in my capacity as president of our business, for example, should I share the information that I have with all family members so that they have the same investment opportunity? If I am on the board of the community bank because I am president of our business and the bank gives me an opportunity to buy stock in its next stock offering, must I share that opportunity with the rest of the family or may I purchase stock on my own? Unless such questions are clarified, such actions and decisions can cause significant resentments in family businesses involving multiple siblings or cousins.

Philanthropy

Philanthropic initiatives provide an excellent opportunity for unifying families when they give family members who are not in the business a larger say than those who are in the business. That gives the "outsiders" a more central role in the whole family. The opposite, of course, is also true—if family members in the business make all the philanthropic decisions, then those not in the business tend to feel even more cut out. It can be a very generous act for those in the business to allow those who are not to have a say on philanthropic decisions.

Developing a philanthropy policy can be difficult. For the policy to work effectively, the family has to agree in some way to unify its giving. If you are going to unify your giving, you have to be unified in other ways as well. Involving family members in philanthropy can also provide them with great training in business strategic thinking and governance. Among the many questions family members will find themselves discussing as they develop philanthropy policy are:

Involving family members in philanthropy can provide them with great training in business strategic thinking and governance.

☛ What values and philosophy underlie our giving? How does our giving support family values and the family mission? To whom or to what shall we give? How focused do we want to be? Should our philanthropic goals coincide with our business goals?

☞How do we give? Who contributes the money? Do we all give separately or must we give together? How do we choose who is in charge of making decisions about giving? What is the process? Will we set up a separate foundation and hire a family member or an outside professional to run it? Do we give as a family or as a business, or as a combination of the two? (Many families strive to make a clear distinction between the business's community relations or marketing-related giving and the family's philanthropy).

☞Are individual family members still expected to make contributions on their own, or is the family creating a unified mechanism so that individual members need not reach into their own pockets?

☞How does our attitude about secrecy versus openness affect our philanthropy? Do we wish to keep quiet about our giving? Or do we want to seek publicity for our giving as a way of benefitting the business? What value do we place on family members taking on leadership positions in the philanthropies we support and being in the public eye?

☞How will we handle controversy? This might mean a controversial gift—such as a donation to an arts group or a religious organization that turns out to offend employees or suppliers or a particular family member. It might mean controversy among family members, each of whom has a favorite charity.

Exit-Redemption/Retirement

Family members need the freedom to exit the business—as an employee or an owner—without feeling that they are leaving the family. A policy can be developed that answers such questions as: Should there be a mandatory retirement age for family members and, if so, what is it? Under what other conditions must or can a family member retire? **What financial mechanisms can we create to provide liquidity to shareholders?** A family may wish to have separate policies—one addressing exit-redemption issues and another addressing retirement.

Should there be a mandatory retirement age for family members and, if so, what is it?

49

Marriage Contracts/Prenuptial Agreements

Wealthier families may want to consider requiring that children have prenuptial agreements, or marriage contracts, as a means of preserving ownership of the business for future generations of the family.

Some of the questions that family members can discuss as they work toward a policy include: What is the purpose of a prenuptial agreement? Is the concern restricted to family business ownership or does it include other assets, too? Of whom should such agreements be required and when? What kind of education about the necessity of marriage contracts is needed by our children and their future spouses and how will we be sure that they get it? How can we avoid the distrust that often surrounds prenuptial agreements? And how can we make our sons- and daughters-in-law feel welcome into the family despite our requirement for prenups? (See Family Business Leadership Series No. 10, *Making Sibling Teams Work: The Next Generation.*)

Dividends or Distributions of Profit

By the second or third generation, not every family member can or should work in the family business. Having a way in which family members can get monetary benefits from the family business other than by working in it becomes very important.

> *By the second or third generation, having a way in which family members can get monetary benefits from the family business other than by working in it becomes very important.*

Paying dividends helps discourage family members from trying to join the business for the wrong reasons.

Questions families will explore as they debate dividend policy include: What purpose are dividends to serve? What effect will different levels of dividends have on the company? For example, how would a certain level of dividend affect growth? How would it be perceived by employees or management? How would it affect their motivation or their commitment to the business? How important is it for the dividend to be stable from year to year or to vary? What will the dividend be? (We've seen policies that stipulate as little as 1% of appraised market value and others that pay out high percentages of net profit.)

Some families emphasize in their policies that family members should not become dependent on dividends to support a certain level of lifestyle. (Of course, some family members pay no attention and do become dependent on dividends anyhow, but at least spelling out the policy helps relieve family business leaders and board members of guilt if they must reduce the dividend.)

A number of families simply adopt a policy that says, "We leave it to the board of directors to determine the appropriate rewards to ownership versus the appropriate capitalization of the business."

A family who chooses to pay lower dividends might open its policy with a statement that says, "Our role as a family is to make sure that the business grows and creates jobs. The purpose of the business is not merely to support our standard of living." (See Family Business Leadership Series No. 7, *Financing Transitions: Managing Capital and Liquidity in the Family Business.*)

Public Relations/Publicity

Some family business owners love publicity not only for their company but for themselves. They see an advantage to their business in appearing personally in company advertising campaigns or by being featured on their companies' websites. But publicity isn't for everyone, or every family business. Some of the questions that policy development on this issue raises are: How do we portray the business in the community? How do we portray it to the outside world? Is prominence in the media important to us?

Some business families make rules about who in the family can talk to the media and under what circumstances. Some require that a request for an interview be cleared by the family. Others say it's fine to appear in the media as long as a family member doesn't discuss certain issues. Still other families insist that if a single member of the family is asked to appear in the media, other family members must also be included.

A family's attitude toward public visibility will be heavily influenced by how secretive or open it is.

A family's attitude toward public visibility will be heavily influenced by how secretive or open it is. If it's a highly secretive family, the policy is easy: nobody communicates with the outside world, or there are strict rules governing how family members do it. Publicity is shunned. If it's a very open family, it may have very few rules about how family members communicate with the outside world and may very actively seek publicity.

Use of the Family Name

For many family businesses, the family name "on the door" becomes prominent and is something to be valued and protected. Consider the Gallo wine family. The wine-making brothers in the family went to court to prevent another brother from putting the Gallo name on a line of cheese. The cheese maker argued that it was his name, too, and he had a right to use it on his cheese. But the judge said he did not, contending that the other brothers had invested enormous sums of money putting the family name on wine. Obviously the wine-making brothers felt the need to protect their interest in the Gallo name.

Anything a family member does that brings attention to a family is a legitimate concern of the family and many families feel they should have a say in such matters.

There are other issues as well. When your family name is prominent in a community, others want you sit on the board of directors of this nonprofit organization or that, or to use your name on their letterhead as a member of their advisory council. Or you may be asked to lend your name as honorary chair of a big fund-raising event or even to endorse a product. One family-business member we know was asked to run for public office. He ran the idea by the family and the family said no. "And I respect my family's decision," he said.

A prominent name can expose a whole family to celebrity and its accompanying risks: possible embarrassment or the uncovering of things about family members' lives or about the business that the family does not want exposed. The matter of security and the exposure of family members to danger is a very real concern to well-known, wealthy family business owners.

Anything a family member does that brings attention to a family is a legitimate concern of the family and many families feel they should have a say in such matters. After all, inappropriate use of the family's name can impact the integrity of both the family and the company.

Loan Programs/Venture Capital

A loan policy addresses a host of questions relating to the passing of money back and forth between a business and family members and others. Who can receive a loan from the business for how much, under what circumstances and with what terms? That's the key question. Who makes the decision and who knows about it?

A loan policy may also determine whether or not a family member can borrow against his or her stock regardless of the origin of the loan—whether it's from the company or from an outside source. The policy will also describe the terms and conditions under which stock can be pledged as collateral or loans can be obtained from the company. Such issues should be part of legally binding shareholder agreements. (See Chapter 5.) Families should carefully think through the consequences and scenarios of allowing family members to obtain outside loans using company stock as collateral. If a lender forecloses on Uncle Hobart, would stock end up outside family control? If Cousin Rosita can't pay back her bank loan, the family business may have to bail her out. That could mean an unplanned, unanticipated hit on the business's capital structure.

Some families decide that they want to design a program that will stimulate entrepreneurship among family members, particularly those with business ideas unrelated to the business. In such cases, the family must determine whether funds will be provided through loans or if the family business can provide venture capital. When the company makes a loan, what interest rate will be charged?

Other questions that need to be answered include: Who will make decisions about what projects get funded? Do we set up some kind of "venture oversight board"? Are we doing this as part of our family business strategic planning? Or is this just to help family members? Does the family member who originally received the loan or venture capital have a right to buy out the whole venture he or she started? Or does the family business itself have the right to buy out the venture?

Still other questions a loan policy might address are: What precedents are we setting when we make a loan? Will loans to family members be limited to business ventures? What if someone wants to borrow from the company to buy a house? What if a key employee wants to borrow money from the company? Is there a cap on the dollar amount anyone can borrow?

Another issue to address is the matter of making loans *to* the business. This allows a family member to lend excess personal cash to the company and be paid a nice interest rate. Who gets the opportunity to do that and under what circumstances?

Company Archives

A family may wish to set forth policy about how and where the history of the family and the business is kept and who is responsible for it—is it a family member, and, if so, is he or she paid? The policy may also address what rights family members have to family heirlooms—for example, who has access to Great Grandmother Roth's portrait, or to the first cigarette lighter the company ever made?

Family Offices

Wealthier business families may wish to set up a family office to manage family wealth through trusts and investments and/or provide "concierge" services to family members, from securing airline reservations to obtaining theater tickets. Some family offices also provide coordinated legal and accounting services for family members. A family may adopt a policy that says, in effect, "As a family, we will retain an attorney," but make it clear that individual family members are not prevented from conferring with their own personal attorneys. The policy might stipulate that family members will be open with one another about estate planning or that "we will be open with those dimensions of our estate planning that relate to the family business." The family office can then coordinate estate planning and other matters.

Family-Business Relations

Some families draw up rules governing the family's use of business resources. It would address such issues as whether family members can use company employees for personal favors or draw on company assets. For example, can I ask an employee in the computer department to help me install a computer for personal use at my home? Can I ask the grounds crew to do some landscaping at my house? Can company mechanics service my personal car?

Can the family make personal use of the company airplane? Of company tickets to sports and theater events? If so, who is allowed to use them? Who can take guests?

What about business trips? Can I take my spouse at company expense?

As you can see, the possibilities for developing policies in a family business are rich and seemingly endless. Some families develop policies not touched upon here—such as policies regarding family members' public service, or guidelines stating what and how financial indicators (such as return on investment or economic value added) will be used to measure business performance and management accountability. Perhaps you have even thought of some topics not mentioned here. If so, we'd like to know!

VII. *One Policy, Two Ways*

Consider two families who want to develop a policy that will offer guidelines for the employment of family members in their respective businesses. Both families operate successful companies, and both are made up of thoughtful people who want the best for their families and their business. Beyond that, they are very different — and so are the policies they develop.

Let's imagine these two scenarios:

SCENARIO #1 - The Goldoni Family

Goldoni Foods is the maker of fresh pastas and sauces sold in upscale food stores in cities along the East Coast. It was founded 30 years ago by Angelo Goldoni, 64, who immigrated with his family from Italy when he was a teenager. Goldoni Foods has 45 employees and, for the past decade or so, Angelo has enjoyed the company of his three sons, Mario, Dino, and Dominick—all vice presidents—in the business. The two oldest children, however, are sisters Gina and Teresa. Angelo did not welcome either of them into Goldoni Foods. In his mind, business was a man's world. He believed women should raise the children and look after their husbands—that was more in keeping with his upbringing.

Being out of the business didn't much bother Gina, who married well and, except for early experience as a secretary, never worked outside the home—a life similar to that of her mother. Teresa, however, resented not being asked to join. A talented young woman now in her mid-30s, Teresa opened her own company—a health-care communications firm—seven years ago and it has been extremely successful. Despite her disappointment about not joining Goldoni Foods, Teresa maintained a good relationship with her family, and they admired what she accomplished—so much so that Mario, with his father's blessing, asked Teresa to join him and her two other brothers in coming up with a family employment policy for Goldoni Foods.

"You know, Gina's oldest boy starts college soon," said Mario. "He's been working for us during the summer and after school, and he's smart. A lot of our children are teenagers or soon will be. We have to start thinking about the next generation."

Teresa agreed to serve on the committee. She had children, too, and maybe one day, they would be interested in joining Goldoni Foods.

The Process

The first meeting of the four siblings got off to a rocky start when Teresa asked her brothers to be open to the idea of allowing their daughters and nieces into the business. Her own experience still stung and she wanted things to be different for the girls in the next generation.

"You know Dad will never go for that," said Dino, who had three sons but no daughters. "He still thinks women should stay home and look after the kids. He'll never change."

"But he did say it was our job to come up with the policy," protested Dominick. He had two daughters and no sons, so he was a little more inclined to hear Teresa's point of view. Besides, his wife was a little like Teresa — holding an executive position at another company — while Dino's wife was more like Gina, preferring not to work outside the home.

"Look," said Mario, who had agreed to serve as chairman of the group, "we don't have to make any decisions today about what the policy will be. Teresa only asked us to be open to the idea. There may be some other issues we want to be open about, too, that Dad may not be happy about. Outside work experience, for example. You know how he thinks that's pointless and how he's always saying a kid can get enough experience working at Goldoni. The point is, we want to do what is best for the business and best for the family."

Dominick volunteered to serve as secretary of the group, taking notes on all the group's discussions. At the first meeting, Mario also asked the group members to come up with a list of issues they wanted the policy to address.

"What about 'Can everybody come into the business?'" suggested Dino. "You know how Dad thinks any male in the family should be able to have a job in the business."

"And what about compensation? Dad has always believed that family members should be paid equally, so that's the policy right now," put in Dominick. "Can we keep on doing that? Should we?"

Shortly, they had a long list of questions. They agreed to break up into teams of two and go visit other family businesses to find out what their experiences were. Teresa also volunteered to get input from Gina and her brothers' wives; she might even talk with Mom. Other assignments were made—someone to talk with experts at several university family business forums; someone to get advice from the family business's lawyer and some other advisors the business relied on.

Goldoni Foods still did not have an outside board of directors—Angelo wouldn't hear of it—so there were no independent board members to bounce ideas off of.

The siblings met once a month for several months, reporting back on what they had learned and, at last, beginning to have some discussion. On the touchy issues, Dino often sided with what he thought his father would want. But when he saw that the other three were convinced that the business should be open to daughters as well as sons—an opinion his wife also shared—he agreed to go along. He was also willing to concede that it might be time to start compensating family members according to market rates—he'd learned from discussions with members of his trade association that that's what many of them were doing. And he was pleased when several members of the group agreed with him that the business should continue to welcome any family member who wanted a job (daughters included, this time).

Teresa and Dino drafted the policy. It was discussed and redrafted several times, and before they were through, they showed the draft policy to the family business advisors and got some additional ideas from them. Finally, the group agreed that they were ready to show it to Dad and the rest of the family.

Angelo, of course, didn't like it. Well, some of it was okay. But that part about letting girls into the business! "Are you crazy?" he sputtered. And that part about compensation being market-based instead of equal? "Some of your kids are going to think you don't love them," he warned.

He had a hard time listening to his sons and daughter. But they had known he would find it tough, so they invited Dad—and anyone else in the family who wanted to come—to a special meeting that included some of Angelo's best business friends. In the end, it was the friends who persuaded Angelo that his children were on the right track and that he should give the policy a chance. "After all," they said, "they and their children are the ones who have to live with it, not you."

"Okay," he sighed. "But I hope I never have to say, 'I told you so.'" And secretly, he was pleased at how well his children had worked together on their own to create the new policy. That gave him more confidence in the future. He was also very touched at how much respect they showed for him and the business he had built.

GOLDONI FOODS
Family Employment Policy

Introduction

Since its founding in 1968 by Angelo Goldoni, Goldoni Foods has stood for quality products, excellent customer service, and integrity. As it has grown to include members of the second generation, the Goldoni family has also taken pride in the fact that Goldoni Foods is a family business. We believe that the business affords the family many opportunities: To serve our community and our customers; to provide financial support for the family; to provide employment not only for family members but also for members of our community outside the family; to offer a learning environment for family members; and to serve as a vehicle for instilling values in our children, our employees, and, by extension, our community.

We believe that to preserve these opportunities and to "live our values," it is desirable to maintain the presence of the Goldoni family in the business. For that reason, all direct descendants of Angelo and Rosa Goldoni (including any adopted children) are welcome to join Goldoni Foods. Family members who are not direct descendants will be considered outside applicants and will be evaluated accordingly.

Employment of direct descendants (hereinafter called family members) shall be conditioned upon the following guidelines:

Requirements for Entry

We recognize two employment "tracks" at Goldoni foods: (1) a professional/management career track requiring higher levels of education, and (2) a track that provides employment in jobs that do not require special training or degrees.

Family members wishing to pursue the professional/management track are expected to obtain the training or education necessary to meet those aspirations. If senior management is the goal, an MBA or other relevant advanced degree is desirable. Before joining Goldoni Foods, family members on the professional/management track are also required to obtain at least three years of successful outside work experience.

Family members who wish to join the business but who do not aspire to professional and management positions are expected to complete a high school education. Attendance at community college and outside work experience are desirable but not mandatory. Those without work experience will begin in entry-level positions. Family members who elect this track will not be eligible for promotion to senior level positions.

Goldoni Foods has a valued reputation for hiring people with disabilities. Any family member with a disability will be encouraged to join the company and may or may not be excluded from the above requirements, depending on his/her abilities.

Family members wishing to join the company should declare their intention by the age of 30 and should have actually joined the company by age 35.

Placement

The decision of where to place a family employee will be made by the Family Management Council (currently consisting of the family vice presidents and president). When possible, it is desirable that one family member not be supervised by another.

Performance

Family members are expected to meet and preferably exceed the level of performance required by the job. To do otherwise leaves the family open to resentment among non-family employees, which is not good for Goldoni Foods.

Family employees who do not meet the required performance level will receive a warning from one of the family vice presidents. If the performance continues to be unsatisfactory, a family employee may be dismissed by a majority vote of the Family Management Council.

Promotions

Family employees and non-family employees will be considered for promotion when positions open. All else being equal, preference will be given to family members.

Compensation

Family employees in the third generation will be compensated at market rates appropriate for their positions. Vacation time and other benefits will be according to standard company rules.

Departure/Re-entry

A family employee who leaves the company voluntarily may return once by the unanimous decision of the Family Management

Council but only if an appropriate position is vacant. No position will be created for a returning family member.

A family member who has been dismissed may return under the same conditions but for a trial period of three months. If performance is satisfactory, he or she may then be retained on a permanent basis.

Part-time/Summer Employment

Younger family members are encouraged to gain the broadest exposure possible to the family business while they are still students. Opportunities for summer jobs, college internships, and part-time work will be made available.

Part-time work and other special arrangements (telecommuting, job-sharing, etc.) for permanent employees will be at the discretion of the employee's supervisor and will be approved by the appropriate vice president.

SCENARIO #2 - The Harlan Family

Harlan Aircraft Supply, based in a Midwestern city, is a third-generation business with 245 employees. There are seven cousins in the business and one of the oldest, Clark Harlan, is president and CEO. Clark, however, is 61. He plans to retire at 65 and believes that the best person to succeed him is a non-family senior manager, Alberto Diaz. His cousins are either too old to be considered for the job or, like the youngest, Mitzi, an engineer, not really interested in being CEO. A few members of the fourth generation are in the business, but they are young and still too inexperienced for top management.

The family is becoming larger and more complex. There are 15 shareholders now, and the fourth generation has just seemed to explode with children—37 at last count. A few of them are high school and college students who work part-time at Harlan Aircraft.

Thanks to the wisdom of Clark's uncles, the second generation to run the business, the family long ago established a family council and a board of directors. In addition to four family members, the board includes three independent directors—all CEOs of other companies.

Clark's cousin, Georgia, a physician, is the leader of the family council. At Clark's urging, Georgia agreed to ask the council to review and redraft the family's employment policy. The policy hadn't been revisited in a long time. "Under the existing rules," Clark told Georgia, "a non-family member isn't allowed to become CEO. That's going to be a problem when I retire." He also felt that the policy needed to put the company in the best position for the challenges it now faced. New growth spurts were expected, and the company was beginning to move aggressively into the global market.

The Process

What the family council members found when they reviewed the existing employment policy was that while it had served the company well for a number of years, some of its stipulations might now inhibit the company. As Clark had pointed out, for example, the policy did indeed state that only a family member could lead the company. It also included a rule against in-laws joining the company, and the council wasn't sure if this was a good rule or a bad one. Much of the decision making about who got hired and who didn't still seemed to rest with the family.

The process that the Harlan family council used was similar to that of the Goldoni family's committee. But the Harlan family had more resources and more infrastructure. Like the Goldonis, the Harlans' family council, as a committee-of-the-whole, did some research and got input from other family members and business advisors. But they also consulted with the board's outside directors. They also had the advantage of being far enough removed from the founder that they weren't intimidated by what they thought the founder's opinions might be.

The family council shared its first draft of a new policy with the board of directors. The board made some suggestions and the council did several more drafts.

Finally, it was ready to go to the entire family. Some members of the family were upset with the new proposals—especially the provision making it possible for a non-family member to become CEO. One or two fretted that now it might not be as easy as in the past for their children to join the company. But others countered that the survival and health of the business were important to the entire family and said the new policy was designed to foster business health.

The family long ago had decided that when matters were brought to the family for a vote, the majority would rule. When a vote was called for on the proposed new employment policy, its proponents prevailed and the policy was adopted. In keeping with a Harlan tradition, every family member eligible to vote signed the new document. Those with reservations about some of its points knew that their concerns would be filed as supporting documents with the policy in the Harlan family's master set of policies.

HARLAN AIRCRAFT SUPPLY
Family Employment Guidelines

Preamble

For half a century, Harlan Aircraft Supply has been a family-owned and family-led company proud of its service to the aircraft industry. It will soon move into the new millennium and into the fourth generation of Harlans, passages which require the establishment of new traditions and new ways of doing things. It is the purpose of this document to set forth guidelines for the employment of family members that will assure the continued health and well-being of the business as it enters a new century and a new era.

General Principles

For the purposes of this document, family members shall be construed to mean shareholders, spouses, children, and legally adopted children of shareholders.

All family members will be regarded as full members of the family and be shown equal love and respect whether or not they join the family business.

Employment in Harlan Aircraft Supply is neither a birthright nor an obligation. Preparation, dedication, effort, demonstrated ability and a desire to work at Harlan Aircraft as well as business needs and economic conditions will all determine the hiring, placement, advancement, and compensation of family members in the company.

It is our intention to attract the most qualified people—family and non-family—to all levels of employment, including senior management. While it is our hope that there will always be family representation in senior management, talented non-family managers should be able to aspire to and be promoted to the highest levels of leadership in order that the best interests of the company will be served.

No jobs will be created solely for the purpose of employing family members, nor will non-family employees be let go to make room for family members.

Preparation

Family candidates must meet the same criteria for hiring as non-family candidates. Generally, this means a minimum of a four-year degree in a relevant field of study, with advanced degrees required for some positions.

Application Process

Family members who desire a position with Harlan Aircraft are expected to go through the normal application process, utilizing the services of the company human resources department.

Performance and Review

Harlan Aircraft expects family employees to meet the same level of performance required of non-family employees. They are also subject to the company's standard performance reviews. Failure to perform satisfactorily will lead to dismissal.

Compensation and Benefits

Compensation will be based on fair market value, as determined by the company Board's Compensation Committee. Benefits will be the same as those offered to non-family employees.

Youth

In order to educate our children about the world of work, the company offers and will continue to offer part-time and summer work for family members who are in high school and college.

Family Employment Committee

A Family Employment Committee will be appointed by the Family Council to (1) work with the Board of Directors and management to create career development opportunities and mentoring opportunities for family employees; (2) educate family members about their roles and responsibilities as family employees; and (3) identify additional ways to expose young family members to and interest them in employment in the family's business.

While both the Goldoni and Harlen families are fictional, they represent real cases. In these scenarios, two very different families with very different cultures and businesses have come up with very different employment policies. But each meets the need of the business-owning family who developed it. The Goldoni policy represents a smaller family going from the first generation to the second, where the entrepreneurial and somewhat-controlling founder still exerts a firm influence. The Harlan policy reflects a much larger business moving from third to fourth generation. The Harlan family is at a stage where it seeks to become ever more professional and objective in its business practices while at the same time recognizing the value of the company to the family and the family to the company.

VIII. *A Word About Implementation*

Sometimes the implementation of a policy goes awry, despite the fact that all the relevant decision makers seem to agree on what the policy would be. One or more family members may deliberately ignore parts or all of a policy. Grandpa, the founding chairman, may see that his 20-year-old grandson gets a job at an out-of-town plant despite the family's agreement that family members can't be hired unless they have minimal levels of education and experience. ("I was just doing the boy a favor," Grandpa will say in self-defense.) Or Elsie may use a marked company van to drive her friends to a bar, despite rules against personal use of company vehicles and the embarrassment to the family—owners of a child development center—at having the van parked outside the bar.

Infractions may occur for one of several reasons. In some cases, family members start finding fault with the implementation because agreement actually has not adequately been reached about the policy and trust is missing. The policy may be fine, but family members start to argue with each other's interpretation of it. It may be that there are deep-seated resentments in the family that need to be resolved. Manuel may feel that his older brother doesn't take him seriously and still thinks of him as a child of 11, for example, or Rhonda may harbor anger over the fact that her brother earns more than she does even though, in her opinion, their jobs are comparable. The family may find it needs to bring in a skilled consultant to help clear up the resentments that are holding the family back.

Sometimes family members have legitimate disagreements about the interpretation of a policy. That's why capturing all the background discussion on paper and filing it with the master policy is so valuable. Then the family can go back and review what was said and what was intended. Sometimes language may need to be re-drafted to give a policy more clarity.

And sometimes, implementation erodes because time has gone by since the policy was adopted, realities have changed, and family members no longer agree on the policy. When that happens, arguing about the policy makes no sense. The family needs to look at what it stood for when it created the policy, consider what has changed, re-ground itself philosophically, and revise the policy to meet the new reality.

Some families set up enforcement mechanisms—a family council or board might be empowered to inform transgressors that they are in violation of a policy and to tell them that their interpretation of the policy is wrong. The council or board can then provide the correct interpretation.

We've known some families, who "excommunicate" dissenting members, literally shutting them out of the business and the family. This is an extreme, but it shows how culture can influence implementation.

Most families avoid such punishments, however. They instead simply use what might be called moral persuasion. When one family member goes astray, the wider family tries to coax that person into conformity. The real issue here is: Does the vast majority of the family share a common view? If so, they can tolerate an individual or a small group being inconsistent, and they can point out infractions in a way that's graceful enough and tasteful enough so that the transgressors do not win sympathy from family members who may be "at the margins" — that is, who may be somewhat indifferent. One way to think about this is to ask yourselves if you can point out infractions in a way that you would be proud for your children to observe.

Another way to exercise moral persuasion when there is a violation of policy is to confront the transgressor with a question. The scenario might go like this:

Family: "Why did you hire Ernie, Grandpa? You know our employment policy sets forth the hiring procedure and you've just gone outside that procedure. Besides, Ernie's not qualified for a job in our company."

Grandpa: "I was just trying to help him and his mom."

Family: "We understand that. But still, you shouldn't be going off and violating the policy all by yourself. We could have found a way to help Ernie and his mom without violating the policy. Next time, let's discuss things first. Then we can find a way to solve a problem and still be consistent with our policies."

In this way, the family reinforces its expectation that family members will adhere to policy and it does so without creating a major fight.

Policy violations can even be looked at as opportunities because they cause family problems to surface. Problems can then be discussed in a constructive way at family meetings or in other venues, thus strengthening family communication.

Another way to deal with infractions is to modify the rules by being more inclusionary and tolerant of the views of transgressors. The family who "excommunicates" dissenters is doing just the opposite— it is being exclusionary. But maybe the rules can be modified so that they cast a wider net and encompass the perspectives of more family members. Such modifications need to be done thoughtfully and consciously, however. The family needs to stay in control of the process.

Except for a shareholder agreement, which is a legal contract, none of your policies will be legally binding (unless constructed that way) and none of them will be stronger than the support that they have within the family. It's therefore up to the family to use its best communication techniques to encourage adherence to its policies. And the best way to do that is to begin long before implementation comes into play, following the process for developing policies described in Chapter 3.

IX. *Summary*

When you and your family take the time to thoughtfully develop policies, you are doing yourselves a favor: You are anticipating problems before they arise and coming up with solutions to handle them. In a sense, it's disaster planning. And sometimes, you can head off the disaster by doing the planning, simply because your family gains skills in working together, communicating, resolving differences, and solving problems. As you build and use these skills, your family becomes stronger and closer.

Families profit immeasurably when they look for creative approaches to policy development. The members of one large, older business that we know wanted to be able to recruit the best family talent available but they were worried that the children of family members who didn't work in the business were being neglected. They felt these particular members of the younger generation might offer a pool of family ability that shouldn't be overlooked and decided to reach out to them. In its employment policy, the family created a section that set up a program of education that would not only help answer questions that younger family members had about the business but also would provide information about jobs they might aspire to. The policy also established a paid internship program that would encourage younger family members to get basic work experience in the company.

In another family, the members of the third generation wanted to make their growing business more professional. One of the steps they wanted to take was to create a policy that would end special perks that family members received—from reserved parking spaces and season football tickets to the use of company cars. They felt such privileges sent the wrong message to non-family employees, creating resentment of family employees. But the senior generation still in the business protested their children's idea. "Our family created this business and we own it," they said. "Why shouldn't we enjoy the

Families profit immeasurably when they look for creative approaches to policy development.

fruits of our labor and the risks we have taken?" Finally, a compromise was reached that satisfied everyone: The senior generation could keep their perks; but beginning with the third generation, special family perks would no longer be available. The family members also agreed to share information about the new policy with non-family employees.

Such creativity ensures that a family thinks through issues thoroughly, which means the solutions are uniquely fitted to the family and business involved.

As you and your family set out to develop policies that will help assure the continued success of your business, promise yourselves that you will not rush the process. Instead, invest the time needed to go through the steps outlined in Chapter 3. When you honor the process, you enhance your chances of not only developing policies that work best in supporting your family and your business, you also increase the prospect for buy-in from the whole family. That buy-in is the best assurance you can have that the policies you have worked so hard to develop will be observed and respected.

Appendices

Appendix A

FAMILY BUSINESS POLICIES TO CONSIDER

Governance

- Criteria for board members
- Make-up of board
- Frequency of family meetings
- Membership criteria for family council or family association
- Funding of family meetings
- Communications and relationships between board and family
- Strategic goals (e.g., growth, debt, etc.) for business
- Selection of professional advisors
- Successor selection process

Employment

- Qualifications
- Conditions (e.g., leaves, part-time, etc.)
- Reporting relationships
- Compensation, benefits, perks and expenses
- Performance review
- Titles
- Severance

Ownership and Financial Planning

- Conditions for ownership and voting rights
- Dispute resolution process
- Dividends
- Redemption process
- Business valuation methodology
- Estate plan communications and coordination and agreements
- Buy-sell agreement (shareholder agreement)
- Insurance plans
- Marriage contract arrangements
- Rights and responsibilities of non-employed owners

- Rules for joint travel
- Addressing family member financial distress

Interpersonal Relationships

- Conflict resolution
- Listening and communicating guidelines
- Decision-making process
- Conduct in public and with each other
- Conflict of interest and non-compete

Appendix B

SAMPLE POLICY: Conflict-of-Interest and Self-Dealing

Lincoln Hardware Distributors and the Lincoln family have long enjoyed a reputation for honesty and integrity—among employees, customers, suppliers, and competitors, and in the community. Since the company was founded in 1971, the family and business have both grown in size and complexity. Several family members and/or their spouses have now founded businesses of their own and others are also considering launching their own enterprises. In light of these developments and in order to preserve the reputation for honesty and integrity that is the legacy of Lincoln Hardware Distributors and the Lincoln family, we hereby adopt, and will abide by, the guidelines below. It is our intent to avoid any conflicts-of-interest, real or perceived.

1. Lincoln Hardware Distributors shall not engage in business with any family member and/or spouse who has his or her own enterprise or who is employed in another company. It is the intent of Lincoln Hardware to use suppliers and service providers who are unrelated to the founding family in any way.

2. Family members, their spouses, and their children, whether or not they work inside the business, will not be permitted to avail themselves of the services or the resources of Lincoln Hardware Distributors for personal use.

3. Family members, their spouses, and their children shall attempt at all times to avoid any perception of impropriety in business matters. Toward that end, family members will not invest in companies that are suppliers to Lincoln Hardware nor seek to benefit financially from information and opportunities gained as a result of their association with Lincoln Hardware.

4. Lincoln Hardware will not intercede on behalf of family members seeking employment with other companies nor in any way pressure or encourage suppliers to hire any member of the Lincoln family.

5. Family members, their spouses, and their children will not be permitted to seek charitable donations from Lincoln Hardware

employees or suppliers or their employees. Fund-raising by family members and relatives at any Lincoln Hardware facility is not permitted. Fund-raising at Lincoln Hardware will be limited to the United Way and to those charitable organizations and causes designated by the Lincoln Hardware Employee Leadership Committee.

6. Copies of the Lincoln Hardware Distributors Conflict-of-Interest Policy will be distributed to all family members, company employees, and suppliers.

Appendix C

SAMPLE POLICY: Philanthropy

Recognizing our legacy as descendants of the founders of the Alvarado Toy Company and wishing to fulfill our sense of obligation to our community and the world in which we live, the six branches of the third generation of the Alvarado family now join together to form a charitable endeavor to be known as the Alvarado Fund. By joining forces, we hope to make a bigger impact with our charitable dollars than we can make individually or as separate branches of the family. We will be guided by the following principles and commitments:

1. The Alvarado Fund will focus its annual giving in the communities where we live in one or more of three areas: children, animals, and the arts.

2. Each of the six branches of the family will contribute $15,000 annually to the Alvarado Fund.

3. It is intended that the Fund serve as a vehicle for direct giving and not as an endowment for earning or raising other funds. A minimum of 95 percent of the Fund's balance will be gifted annually. Any remaining funds can be used for administrative expenses as needed or added to gifts to be distributed in following years.

4. A rotating Grants Committee, to change annually, will research and make recommendations for each year's recipient(s). The committee, initially chosen by lottery, will consist of two direct Alvarado descendants and one spouse (or, in the case of unmarried descendants, domestic partners of at least two year's duration), or two spouses (or domestic partners) and one descendant. In no case shall the committee consist of three descendants or three spouses/domestic partners. The existing committee will select the succeeding committee. Each committee will choose its own chair.

5. It is the intent of the Alvarado Fund to seek out worthy recipients and not to entertain requests for funding. It is expected that the Grants Committee will be discreet in its activities and present the members of the Fund with a strong, strategic rationale for its selections.

6. Members of the Fund will make the final selection by a simple majority vote.

7. As of the establishment of the Fund, membership consists of 11 senior members of the third generation of the Alvarado Toy Company business-family: six direct descendants, four spouses, and one domestic partner. Children of the founding members of the Alvarado Fund will be invited to join the Fund when they reach the age of 25. They are free to join or not join, as they wish.

8. Each family branch will determine on its own how to put together its annual $15,000 contribution.

9. Each member of the Fund is free to make additional charitable donations outside the Fund or not, as he or she wishes.

10. The members of the Fund do not and will not seek publicity for the giving they do through the Fund. Members of the Fund believe the Fund can do its work more effectively without media attention. If the media approaches the Fund, however, the current chair of the Grants Committee will serve as spokesperson for the Fund.

11. The Alvarado Fund is separate and apart from the corporate charitable activities of the Alvarado Toy Company. Giving decisions of one should not influence the other.

12. It is the desire of the members of the Alvarado Fund that their children be instilled with philanthropic values and be educated in philanthropic matters. The Fund, as an organization, will seek ways to provide such education to the Alvarado children.

13. Fund members will elect a president, a vice president, a secretary, and a treasurer to oversee the business of the Fund. Each officer shall have a term of three years.

14. Fund members may from time to time increase or decrease the annual dollar requirement paid into the Fund by family branches, or may decrease or waive the requirement of a given branch for reasons of hardship. Such decisions require a two-thirds majority vote.

15. The Fund will be administered by Fund members themselves as an unpaid, volunteer activity.

16. Any branch that does not make its required contribution loses it rights to participation in the Fund for that year. If a branch does not participate for five or more years it must pay the current year's contribution plus the prior two years' contributions to participate.

Index

85

The Authors

Craig E. Aronoff, Ph.D., holds the Dinos Eminent Scholar Chair of Private Enterprise and is professor of management at Kennesaw State University (Atlanta). Co-founder of **The Family Business Consulting Group, Inc.** and recipient of the Family Firm Institute's Beckhard Award for outstanding contributions to family business practice, he has spoken to family business audiences on every continent. Aronoff founded and directs the Kennesaw State University Cox Family Enterprise Center, which focuses on education and research for family businesses; its programs have been emulated by more than 100 universities worldwide. Aronoff's undergraduate degree is from Northwestern University, Masters from the University of Pennsylvania, and Ph.D. in organizational communication from the University of Texas.

Joseph H. Astrachan, Ph.D., a principal of **The Family Business Consulting Group, Inc.,** is the Wachovia Chair of Family Business, professor of management and entrepreneurship, Director of the Family Business Academy, and Research Director of the Cox Family Enterprise Center at the Coles College of Business, Kennesaw State University (Atlanta). He is Distinguished Research Scholar at Loyola University Chicago's business school where he directs the research efforts of their well-known Family Business Center. Editor of *Family Business Review,* a scholarly publication of the Family Firm Institute, Astrachan received the lifetime achievement award for his research on family business from the International Family Business Program Association. Astrachan earned his B.A., M.A., M. Phil., and Ph.D. at Yale University, where he studied in the School of Organization and Management.

John L. Ward, Ph.D., co-founder of **The Family Business Consulting Group, Inc.**, is Clinical Professor of Family Enterprises at Northwestern University's Kellogg Graduate School of Management. He is a regular visiting lecturer at two European business schools. He has also previously been associate dean of Loyola University Chicago's Graduate School of Business, and a senior associate with Strategic Planning Institute (PIMS Program) in Cambridge, Massachusetts. Recipient of the Family Firm Institute's Beckhard Award for outstanding contributions to family business practice, he has consulted with family firms around the world, and addressed family business audiences on every continent. A graduate of Northwestern University (B.A) and Stanford Graduate School of Business (M.B.A. and Ph.D.), his *Keeping the Family Business Healthy* and *Creating Effective Boards for Private Enterprises* are leading books in the family business field.

The best information resources for business-owning families and their advisors

The Family Business Leadership Series
Concise guides dealing with the most pressing challenges and significant opportunities confronting family businesses.

Comprehensive — Readable — Thoroughly Practical
- *Family Business Succession: The Final Test of Greatness*
- *Family Meetings: How to Build a Stronger Family and a Stronger Business*
- *Another Kind of Hero: Preparing Successors for Leadership*
- *How Families Work Together*
- *Family Business Compensation*
- *How to Choose & Use Advisors: Getting the Best Professional Family Business Advice*
- *Financing Transitions: Managing Capital and Liquidity in the Family Business*
- *Family Business Governance: Maximizing Family and Business Potential*
- *Preparing Your Family Business for Strategic Change*
- *Making Sibling Teams Work: The Next Generation*
- *Developing Family Business Policies: Your Guide to the Future*
- *Family Business Values: How to Assure a Legacy of Continuity and Success*
- *More Than Family: Non-Family Executives in the Family Business*
- *Make Change Your Family Business Tradition*
- New guides on critical issues published every six to twelve months

The Family Business ADVISOR Monthly Newsletter

Family Business Sourcebook II
Edited by Drs. Aronoff and Ward with Dr. Joseph H. Astrachan, *Family Business Sourcebook II* contains the best thoughts, advice, experience and insights on the subject of family business. Virtually all of the best-known experts in the field are represented.

Now Available:
John Ward's Groundbreaking Family Business Classics
- *Keeping The Family Business Healthy*
- *Creating Effective Boards For Private Enterprises*

For more information:
Family Enterprise Publishers, P.O. Box 4356, Marietta, GA 30061
Tel: 800-551-0633 or 770-425-6673